IN THE ARMS OF HIS LOVE

A Guide to Growing Closer to the
Savior and Receiving His
Unconditional Love

By

Steven A. Cramer

Covenant
Communications, Inc.

CONTENTS

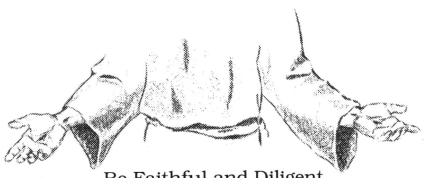

Be Faithful and Diligent
in Keeping the Commandments
of God and I Will Encircle Thee
In the Arms of My Love
(D&C 6:20)

Preface

Elizabeth Sherrill lived on the edge of town, her home surrounded by woods. One day a strange clunking sound in the yard caused her to look out the window where she saw a skunk running helter skelter, zigzagging across her lawn. Stuck on his head was a six-ounce plastic yogurt container.

Running frantically, the skunk struck a rock and whirled in another direction only to crash into the picnic table. Each time he collided with something, he would step back and shake his head violently, trying desperately to free himself. Despairing of freedom, he ran blindly into the woods.

Elizabeth stared after him in dismay, wondering how long it had been since he had forced his head into that carton to reach some bit of food on the bottom. How long had he been running in darkness and terror?

She felt an urge to help the poor creature, but her mind recoiled in revulsion. Could she even find him, much less catch him in his frantic dash through the woods? And even if she could, surely, in his panic he would spray her before she could remove the carton. No, she reasoned, as sorry as she felt for him, it was unthinkable to even try. She tried to forget the skunk as she busied herself with work she needed to do. But the same Lord, who proclaimed that not even a lowly sparrow can fall to the ground unnoticed, was also concerned for this skunk.

Through the influence of his Spirit, Elizabeth's urge to help grew stronger and more insistent. Finally, with no specific plan in mind, and scarcely considering the implications of her decision, she left her house and ran up the driveway to the road. When she'd last seen the frightened skunk, he had run into the woods in the opposite direction. Nevertheless, guided by the Spirit, she dashed down the street as though rushing to a long-ordained appointment. A hundred yards down the road a black-and-white streak emerged from the bushes and ran straight toward her, the carton bumping the pavement with each step.

There was no time to consider the astonishment she felt at finding the skunk so quickly. Extending her arms, she stooped down and grabbed the yogurt carton with both hands.

Unexpectedly strong, the animal tugged and twisted, frantic to escape this new peril. Clawing at the slippery yellow plastic, his body strained backward while Elizabeth pulled in the opposite direction, amazed at the carton's vise-like grip. Finally his small black head popped free.

Elizabeth said, "There we stood, facing each other, two feet apart. I don't know what he saw, or how threatening I appeared, but what I saw was a sharp quivering nose, two small round ears, and alert black eyes that stared straight into mine. For fully ten seconds we held each other's gaze. Then the skunk turned, ran a few yards and vanished into the mouth of a culvert that runs beneath the road." (Elizabeth Sherrill, Contributing Editor, *Guidepost Magazine*, February, 1989, p. 53.)

I love this story because, for me, it symbolizes the arms of Christ's love which are perpetually extended toward us in spite of our failures. Because of the mistakes of the past, many people fear to approach the Lord. Like the frightened skunk who crashed into barriers he couldn't see or understand, we too go from failure to failure, frightened by our inability to understand and solve our spiritual problems. Sometimes we may even feel as repulsive and unwanted as a skunk. But the truth is that the moment we slow our downward plunge and turn toward the Lord, we will find our Savior beckoning to us with arms wide in a loving invitation to come to him.

> Behold, he sendeth an invitation unto all men, for the arms of mercy are extended towards them, and he saith: Repent, and I will receive you. (Alma 5:33.)

The scriptures testify that every person can have the privilege of experiencing these arms of love and mercy. In the chapters that follow we will explore his incredible love, we will gain confidence that his invitation is real and available to every person, and then we will identify a process for bringing each one of us into the arms of his love with total acceptance and fellowship.

Isaiah declared that when we think of Jesus Christ, one of the first names that should come to mind is "Wonderful." (See Isaiah 9:6.) The purpose of this book is to describe his "wonderful" arms of love, his unceasing determination to remove from our lives everything that is imperfect and unworthy, and then escort us triumphantly into the presence of our Father and Mother in heaven.

My desire is that this book will persuade each reader that the Savior's arms of love are extended toward every person, and that he is eager to become our personal friend, companion and guide. I also desire to find the words to convey my appreciation and reverential awe for the Savior's majesty and glory, and for his willingness to be part of our daily lives. I pray that the Lord will use these humble words to guide each of us into the arms of his love.

Part One

A Profile of
His Love

The Arms of His Love

So foolish was I, and ignorant: I was as a beast before thee. Nevertheless I am continually with thee: thou hast holden me by my right hand. Thou shalt guide me with thy counsel, and afterward receive me to glory. (Psalms 73:22-24.)

I the Lord have called thee in righteousness, and will hold thine hand . . . (Isaiah 42:6.)

One of the most breathtaking invitations in all of scripture is found early in the Doctrine and Covenants, wherein the Lord Jesus Christ promised, "Be faithful and diligent in keeping the commandments of God, and I will encircle thee in the arms of my love." (D&C 6:20.)

Satan would have us believe that this wonderful promise is too good to be true, that it is beyond the possibility of ordinary disciples and that it is only theological symbolism and not real. Each chapter in this book, however, will demonstrate that the Savior's promise is true, that it is literal, and that it is available to every person who will make its fulfillment a priority in their life. Many people who love the Savior have accepted this invitation and have experienced the embrace of Christ's strong, loving arms, and so can you.

As a representative of Jehovah (the premortal Christ), the Prophet Lehi testified that he had personally tested the promise of loving arms and found it both true and literal. "The Lord hath redeemed my soul from hell," he said. "I have beheld his glory, and I am encircled about eternally in the arms of his love. He hath filled me with his love, even unto the consuming of my flesh." (2 Nephi 1:15; 4:21.) Glen L. Pace of the Presiding Bishopric validated Lehi's testimony when he said, "Our Lord and Savior Jesus Christ knows you intimately. He knows your name and he knows your pain. If you will approach your Father in Heaven with a broken heart and contrite spirit, you will find yourself miraculously lifted into the loving and comforting arms of the Savior." (*Ensign*, November 1987, p. 41.)

The prophet Mormon also testified that this invitation from the Savior is literal and not just a figure of speech. Speaking of future generations who would look back at the foolish Book of Mormon people who were so needlessly destroyed, Mormon prophesied that we "will sorrow for the calamity of the house of Israel; yea, they will sorrow for the destruction of this people; they will sorrow that this people had not repented that they might have been clasped in the arms of Jesus." (Mormon 5:11.) If this promise has not yet been fulfilled in our own lives, we must ask ourselves what foolish worldliness have we allowed to prevent ourselves from being "clasped" and "encircled" in the arms of his love. As Mormon witnessed the final destruction of his people at the hill Cumorah, he once again lamented over the tragedy of their rejection of Christ's invitation to experience the arms of his love. Consider how his words might apply to us today.

> And my soul was rent with anguish, because of the slain of my people, and I cried: "O ye fair ones, how could ye have departed from the ways of the Lord! O ye fair ones, how could ye have rejected that Jesus, who stood with open arms to receive you!" (Mormon 6:16-17.)

A formerly excommunicated woman gave me permission to share the following experience. Although she had long since repented and had been rebaptized, she couldn't find the peace she longed for and deserved. She said,

I prayed constantly for relief, but the relief didn't come, and I wondered how I could continue life with this weight. What was I going to do? I was totally overcome with sorrow. Finally, one night I left my house so my sobs wouldn't wake my children. I ran through the cold, dark, windy night, pleading for relief. I couldn't bear this guilt anymore. Surely he would help me.

"Exhausted, I returned to my porch, and while sitting there in despair, I felt my Savior's embrace, the warmth of his bosom, the full essence of the forgiveness and love that he had for me. The pain and anguish floated from my body and has never once returned in seven years.

The Savior is anxious to share this blessing with each person. But many of us root our self-image in the mistakes of the past, blocking the Savior's love and preventing ourselves from experiencing his love and peace. But we can discover for ourselves how perfect and non-judgmental the Lord's love really is.

A legitimate way to increase your self-esteem is to become aware that God loves you as you are at this moment. What you have done in the past in no way diminishes his love for you. It is unconditional love; there are no if's or but's attached.

If your feelings about yourself are largely negative, you can change them . . . by realizing that your Heavenly Father [and Savior] love you unconditionally. (Joseph C. Bentley, *The Instructor*, November 1969, p. 399.)

The Lord's unconditional love is difficult for mortals to comprehend because of the imperfections of our own ability to love. Even Elder Neal A. Maxwell said, "I am stunned at his perfect, unconditional love of all." (*New Era*, December 1976, p. 10.) For most of us, the perfect, unconditional, unwavering love of God is incomprehensible and often unbelievable because, according to Paul, "the love of Christ . . . passeth knowledge." (Ephesians 3:19.) Try as we may, we feel utterly incapable of describing something so vast, so pure and selfless, so infinite and perfect and all-encompassing.

God's infinite love simply cannot be reduced to the confinement of mortal words. Yet Paul frequently urged his converts to try and "comprehend with all saints what is the breadth, and length, and depth, and height; And to know the love of Christ, which passeth knowledge, that ye might be filled with all the fullness of God." (Ephesians 3:18-19.) He often prayed that "the Lord [would] direct [their] hearts into the love of God." (2 Thessalonians 3:5.) In other words, while we cannot fully comprehend the perfect, unconditional love of God intellectually, we may each know and experience it emotionally when we allow the Savior to encircle us in the arms of his love.

Lisa A. Johnson, of the *New Era* editorial staff, described the Savior's love as "a deep enduring feeling that seems to warm your entire soul. The kind of sensation that makes you feel as if the heavens have opened and a loving God is encircling you in celestial arms. Sometimes," she said, "it comes as a result of long, hard, concentrated effort. Other times it surprises us, and softly enfolds us when we least expect it." ("I Feel The Savior's Love When . . ." *New Era*, March 1990, p. 20.)

In the scriptures we are exhorted to seek for his mercy and stay in the arms of his love: "Keep yourselves in the love of God, looking for the mercy of the Lord Jesus Christ unto eternal life." (Jude 1:21.)

How often the Lord has invited, indeed, commanded that we must come to him as a little child. And what do we do to receive a child and manifest love for them? We take them in our arms and embrace them. And that is exactly what Christ did with the children brought to him. "And they brought young children to him, that he should touch them." (Mark 10:13.) Thinking that Jesus wouldn't want to be bothered with children, "his disciples rebuked those that brought them. But when Jesus saw it, he was much displeased, and said unto them, Suffer the little children to come unto me, and forbid them not: for of such is the kingdom of God. And he took them up in his arms, put his hands upon them, and blessed them." (Mark 10:14, 16.)

Today we teach our children to sing of that day of glory and reward when the Savior will say, "You've served me well, my little child; Come into my arms to stay." (Mirla Greenwood Thayne, "When He Comes Again".) But the message of scripture is that we do not need to wait until the end of life to feel the embrace of those kind, loving arms. "Be faithful and diligent in keeping the commandments of God and I will encircle thee in the arms of my love." (D&C 6:20.) A young girl related how the stress of school and other pressures drove her to the scriptures for comfort. She said that as she read of his love she felt overwhelmed by the Spirit. "I could truly feel the Lord put his arms around me like a father would comfort a distressed child."

There were two "distressed" children in Denmark who needed and received the comfort of the Savior's arms of love. Their mother, Mette Hansen, was hit by a car while riding her bicycle home from work. For five hours she lay in a hospital, unable to contact her two small children. She was supposed to pick them up from a day-care center. In desperation she pleaded with the Lord to let her children know she was all right and to give them peace and protection, which is exactly what he did.

When Sister Hansen arrived home at 10:15 P.M., she found her two children sitting peacefully on the doorstep. They found their way home, but because they didn't have a key to get into the apartment, they had knelt on the doormat and said a prayer and then sat on the steps waiting for their mother. "And then a nice thing happened to me," her son said. "I felt a big, warm hand touching the top of my head, and I heard a friendly voice saying, 'Your mother is well . . . . It will be a while before she comes home, and it will be dark outside, but just stay calm.' " (*Ensign*, July 1990, p. 62.) Once again the Savior's arms of love reached out to bless those in need.

Yea, they were encircled about with everlasting darkness and destruction; but behold, he has brought them into his everlasting light, yea, into everlasting salvation; and they are encircled about with the matchless bounty of his love. (Alma 26:15.)

The Savior longs to encircle each of us in the arms of his love, but he is often restrained by our discouragement and unbelief. The Prophet Joseph Smith once had a vision in which he saw nine of the twelve apostles in a foreign land. He saw them standing in a circle without shoes. They had been beaten. They were tattered and discouraged, looking at the ground in despair. Standing above them in the air was the Savior, reaching toward them, yearning to lift them, comfort, strengthen, and encourage them with the arms of his love. But they did not see him nor discern his presence. The Savior looked upon them and wept.

It is said that the Prophet could never relate this vision without weeping himself. Speaking of this deep emotion, Truman G. Madsen asked, "Why? Why should he be so touched? Because Christ willingly came to the earth so that the Father's family could come to him boldly, knowing that he knows what is taking place in us when we sin, that he knows all our feelings and cares. The greatest tragedy of life," he said, "is that, having paid that awful price of suffering 'according to the flesh that his bowels might be filled with compassion,' (see Alma 7:11-13) and being now prepared to reach down and help us, he is forbidden because we won't let him. We look down instead of up." (*The Highest In Us*, Salt Lake City, Utah: Bookcraft, Inc., 1978, p. 85.)

A friend told of her experience which occurred when she was in great distress, struggling to repent and overcome actions in her life that were unworthy of a disciple of Christ. She said, "I had been feeling so empty, shallow and lost within. I felt very discouraged. I felt that I wasn't getting through to the Lord. I felt lost and helpless."

After long, intensive prayer, she felt his arms reach down to love and comfort her. "I could actually feel the Savior's love and his compassion. The whisperings of the Spirit came into my mind and my heart: 'I love you. I am here. I have not left you. I know you've made mistakes along the way, but I love you and I know you can do better. Keep going. Don't give up now. You can win the fight. I am here to help you. You are not alone.'" She continued, "As I felt and received this witness and presence of the

Savior's love, there were no harsh feelings of sternness. It was a warm and gentle feeling, like a nudge pushing me forward and onward. Simply a sweet, very loving, compassionate, gentle feeling of embrace, understanding, love, and acceptance. He literally put his arms around my heart and embraced me. Although it was not physical in the sense of flesh and bones, I felt my heart being embraced by the Savior."

Another lady told me how her trials and sorrows led her to the arms of his love, so eagerly extended in compassion and comfort. She said that on one particularly difficult night, "I woke up crying, but with the feeling I was being held gently but securely in Father's arms."

> And thus . . . we see that his arm is extended to all people who will repent and believe on his name. (Alma 19:36.)

October 24th, 1986 was a tragic day in the life of five-year-old Sage Volkman, but like many circumstances of adversity, her suffering led her right into the arms of the Savior. Sage's father, Michael Volkman had taken Sage and her older brother fishing only six days after they had joined the Church. Leaving Sage safely asleep in her sleeping bag in their camping trailer, Michael took eight-year-old Avery with him early the next morning to set their fishing lines in the lake nearby.

As the sky grew lighter, Michael slipped back to the trailer to check on Sage. All seemed well, but only five minutes later their dogs began to bark, and he turned to see billows of black smoke rising above their campsite. After racing the 150 yards in panic, he found the trailer engulfed in flames.

Throwing open the door, he searched frantically through the melting sleeping bags for his daughter. Smoke and flames forced him to retreat, gasping for air, but he threw himself back into the camper, digging through handfuls of burning polyester until he found Sage's lifeless body.

Ignoring the burns on his own face and hands, he dragged Sage out of the inferno and immediately started CPR and artificial resuscitation. For over three minutes

Sage remained lifeless, but he continued his frantic efforts to revive his little daughter, now burned beyond recognition. At last they heard a little squeak and saw her chest heave.

Sage's brother, Avery, who had been praying for his little sister, suddenly noticed the propane tanks on the side of the camper. "Dad," he said, "I think we'd better move." Michael nodded and painfully pulled Sage farther from the trailer. Seconds later the propane tanks exploded.

Later, when Sage was wheeled into the burn unit, the medical staff had little hope of saving her. She had third and fourth-degree burns on her face, arms, chest, and legs. Her nose and one ear had been melted off. Her fingers were so charred that they had to be amputated. One lung had collapsed and the other was barely functioning. A quart of soot was extracted from them.

Perhaps it was an intervention of divine kindness that Sage lapsed into a coma for the next six weeks as she hovered precariously on the verge of death. The doctors emphasized that if Sage did survive, they would expect her to suffer severe brain damage, loss of vision, chronic lung problems, inability to walk, and probably a major loss of hearing. Anything short of that would be a miracle.

God had just such a miracle in mind, however, and through the power of priesthood administration, she was blessed with the strength to overcome the trauma and achieve a full recovery. She came out of her coma one day as her mother was lying on the bed with her. Looking into her daughter's ruined face, she said, "Oh, I love you Sage."

"I love you, too," Sage whispered back, her first response in six weeks.

Finally out of her coma, Sage began to improve. She started breathing on her own. Though it was painful to move her scarred mouth, she slowly learned how to speak again.

Perhaps the hardest thing for Sage was losing her fingers, which she had hoped would grow back as her hair did. Her favorite activity before the fire was drawing, and she missed it terribly. But she was given a computer and has become a whiz at using it to print pictures and play games.

Today Sage attends school, she walks, breathes, smiles and has even learned to ride a bicycle. Though severely disfigured for life, Sage's sweet spirit radiates through her scars. She is an inspiration to all who have the honor of knowing her.

But the highlight of this story is what Sage reported to her family after she came out of the coma. During one of her first priesthood blessings, at the beginning of the coma, she was told, "Go where it is safe—into Heavenly Father's arms." Her family clung to the hope that such could be possible for her, and months later, when Sage learned to talk again, her mother asked Sage if she remembered anything from those first six weeks while she was in coma. Sage said yes, she remembered being with Jesus.

A little skeptical, her mother asked, "What did he say?"

Sage replied, "He just held me and told me he was sorry that I was hurt. He told me he loved me." ("Sage's Song," *Ensign*, August 1989, pp. 30-35.)

George Pace testified:

> The greatest reality of my life is to know that Jesus Christ loves us as a loving father; and that he is anxious to relate to us accordingly. Throughout the scriptures he talks about his relationship with us in a warm, personal way.
>
> On the mount of Olives, he said, "O Jerusalem, Jerusalem, thou that killest the prophets . . . how often would I have gathered thy children . . . as a hen gathered her chickens under her wings, and ye would not! (Matthew 23:37.)
>
> I believe he is saying he would like to put his arms around all of us and comfort and strengthen us. He would like to reach into our hearts, pull out the anxiety, sorrow, and concern and instill in our hearts great peace, joy, and a realization that we are infinitely precious in his eyes. ("What It Means To Know Christ," *Ensign*, September 1974, p. 48.)

The Arms of Kindness

As Nephi viewed a rerun of Lehi's vision of the Tree of Life, he was asked by the angel, "Knowest thou the condescension of God?" (1 Nephi 11:16.) In answer to his own question, the angel then portrayed the incomprehensible kindness shown by the Savior as he left his throne of glory and exaltation to be born to a poor maiden of Nazareth. As the vision of Christ's life continued, Nephi was allowed to view his kindness as he went among the multitudes, moved with compassion, healing all manner of sickness and disease, and freeing the people from the influence of evil spirits. (see 1 Nephi 11:17-31.)

And then, as the ultimate act of condescension and kindness, he allowed himself to be "taken by the people; yea, the Son of the everlasting God was judged of the world . . . . And I, Nephi, saw that he was lifted up upon the cross and slain for the sins of the world." (1 Nephi 11:32-33.) When Jesus Christ placed his arms on that cross and allowed wicked men to nail him there, it was an act of divine kindness to an undeserving world. Someone has said that "It was not the nails that held Jesus to the cross, but his love for you and I."

Prophets through time have expressed amazement at the kindness Christ would show in response to the cruel treatment heaped upon him. Nephi, for example, testified that "the world, because of their iniquity, shall judge him to be a thing of naught; wherefore they scourge him, and he suffereth it; and they smite him, and he suffereth it. Yea, they spit upon him, and he suffereth it." And why did Jesus endure such undeserved indignities? Nephi answers that it is "because of his loving kindness and his long-suffering towards the children of men." (1 Nephi 19:9.)

Two other scriptures mentioning his kindness come to mind:

Rend your heart, and not your garments, and turn unto the Lord your God: for he is gracious and merciful, slow to anger, and of great kindness. (Joel 2:13.)

But thou art a God ready to pardon, gracious and merciful, slow to anger, and of great kindness. (Nehemiah 9:17.)

The scriptures often link Christ's kindness with his patience and forgiveness. Christ is a God of inflexible justice, but that justice is always tempered with mercy. When our repentance allows him to do so, Christ will always show kindness as he leads us from our sins, "for he is kind unto the unthankful and to the evil." (Luke 6:35.) Indeed, said the Savior to a wayward people who had required discipline to bring them to repentance, "In a little wrath I hid my face from thee for a moment; but with everlasting kindness will I have mercy on thee, saith the Lord thy Redeemer." (Isaiah 54:8.)

When Jehovah declares that his kindness is "everlasting" he means exactly that. It is unwavering, dependable, always there when we allow him to manifest it on our behalf. In the words of Enoch's praise, "And were it possible that man could number the particles of the earth, yea, millions of earths like this, it would not be a beginning to the number of thy creations." And yet, declared Enoch, although the Lord has the affairs of the entire universe to administer, "thou art merciful and kind forever." (Moses 7:30.)

The Book of Mormon contains a moving illustration of Christ's kind attention to the feelings of others. As the Nephites anxiously awaited the signs of the Savior's birth, the unbelievers set aside a day after which, if the signs did not appear, all who believed in Christ would be put to death. (See 3 Nephi 1:1-9.) In his concern for this terrible threat upon the members of the church, Nephi spent the entire day in prayer on behalf of the safety of his people. In response to this selfless devotion came a marvelous manifestation of the Savior's kindness:

> And behold, the voice of the Lord came unto him, saying:
> Lift up your head and be of good cheer; for behold, the time is at hand, and on this night shall the sign be given, and on the morrow come I into the world, to show unto the world that I will fulfill all that which I have caused to be spoken by the mouth of my holy prophets.
> And behold, the time is at hand, and this night shall the sign be given. (3 Nephi 1:12-14.)

In the very act of leaving his throne of glory to come to earth and begin his mortality in a lowly stable birth, Jesus Christ took the time to personally answer Nephi's prayer. In just a few hours the signs would have appeared anyway, so why did he detour from his destiny in Bethlehem to give Nephi a personal, vocal revelation. It was because of his tender kindness. "How excellent is thy lovingkindness, O God!" (Psalms 36:7.)

We are told that the Millennial reign will be filled with our praise of the Savior's many acts of kindness. "And now the year of my redeemed is come; and they shall mention the loving kindness of their Lord, and all that he has bestowed upon them according to his goodness, and according to his loving kindness, forever and ever." (D&C 133:52.)

Let us respond to this divine kindness with honor, being careful never to abuse or defile it by deliberately doing things that would offend and hurt our Savior. We need to remember that while his bowels are filled with compassion, mercy, patience, kindness and forgiveness for every sincerely repentant person, he has declared firmly that he will not be mocked by hypocrisy or deliberate indifference.

> O hope of ev'ry contrite heart,
> O joy of all the meek,
> To those who fall, how kind thou art!
> How good to those who seek!
> ("Jesus, the Very Thought of Thee,"
> *LDS Hymns*, 1985, p.141.)

The Arms of Compassion

Blessed be God, even the Father of our Lord Jesus Christ, the Father of mercies, and the God of all comfort; Who comforteth us in all our tribulation. (2 Corinthians 1:3-4.)

One of the saddest questions in all of scripture was asked by the Savior's closest disciples one afternoon when, at the conclusion of a lengthy sermon, Jesus asked them to take him to the other side of the Sea of Galilee. We don't know the size of their ship, but we do know it was a large fishing vessel with mast and sail, and that it was large enough to draw Mark's contrast to "the little ships" some of the crowd used to try and follow them across the sea.

Exhausted from his labors, the Savior found a place to rest at the stern of the ship and quickly fell asleep on a pillow. There is great significance in this, because it demonstrates the humanness of the Savior, that he was mortal and subject to the same needs of the flesh that we have. Without food he hungered; without water he thirsted. And without sleep he tired from his labors, subject to the same fatigue that we experience: "And lo, he shall suffer temptations, and pain of body, hunger, thirst, and fatigue, even more than man can suffer, except it be unto death." (Mosiah 3:7.)

As the ship sailed toward the other side, there arose a great storm of ferocious wind. Such storms were rather fre-

15

quent on the Sea of Galilee. The water lies over six hundred feet below sea level and is surrounded by hills and mountains. As the cooler air from above rushes down upon the warmer water, great windstorms are created. And this storm was of particular power, because even though these men were seasoned fishermen, they were terrified.

And now we can see the significance of Mark mentioning the size of the ship because, as large as it was, the huge waves still poured into it, filling it faster than the disciples could bail. The ship was in danger of breaking apart or sinking.

There is a parallel here to the great storms of turmoil and adversity which sweep into our own lives from time to time; emotional storms that threaten to engulf and destroy us with their discouraging power. Too often we react to these storms with doubt, fear, and distrust, just as the disciples did. Realizing that they were helpless to save themselves, the disciples waded to the stern of the boat to wake the Savior, who was still peacefully asleep. They roused him with this pitiful question:

"Master, carest thou not that we perish?" (Mark 4:38.)

It is a biting, accusatory question, expressing their doubt of his love and concern for them. They could have said, "Lord, please wake up, we need your help," or "Lord, we're in trouble, the boat is about to sink. Can you help us? Will you save us?" But they didn't.

"Master, carest thou not that we perish?"

What this question really asks is, "Why don't you care about our problem? Here we are trying to serve you and we are about to be destroyed. Why are you letting this happen to us?" And haven't we all questioned God in the same way during some trouble or crisis in our own lives? "Why me, Lord? What did I do to deserve this? Why are you letting this happen to me? Where are you? I need you. Why don't you care about what's happening to me?" That Peter learned better is shown later when he taught the disciples that they should be continually "Casting all your care upon him; for he careth for you." (1 Peter 5:7.)

I think the Savior was wounded by their doubts and accusations. "Why are ye so fearful?" he asked. "How is it that ye have no faith?" (Mark 4:40.) In other words, "How can you doubt my love and concern? You've been with me all these months and you have seen my compassion and concern for the suffering of my brothers and sisters. Where is your faith? When will you learn that you can trust me and count on my help in any circumstance or problem? When will you learn that my Father and I will never ignore you or neglect you? We will never let you down. No matter what happens, we will be part of it with you, showing our compassion and love."

The Savior arose and stilled the violent storm with three words: "Peace, be still." The astonished disciples marveled and wondered at the miracle. "What manner of man is this, that even the wind and the sea obey him?" they asked each other. (Mark 4:41.) It is an important question for each of us to answer as well. What manner of Savior do we know? Is he a far-away shepherd, someone who existed two thousand years ago on the pages of scripture? A God who is far away in space, sitting on the throne next to Heavenly Father, separated from us by billions of light years? Is he a God so busy with running the universe that he has no time nor compassion for us? Or do we know Christ as a shepherd who is close to us, just on the other side of the veil, a God who is reaching out with arms of compassion and love? "Cast thy burden upon the Lord, and he shall sustain thee: he shall never suffer the righteous to be moved." (Psalms. 55:22.)

When asked to describe the purpose of his ministry and mission, the Savior explained that Heavenly Father had sent him to reveal their love, compassion, and desire to help us out of our difficulties. "He hath sent me to heal the brokenhearted, to preach deliverance to the captives, and recovering of sight to the blind, to set at liberty them that are bruised." (Luke 4:18.)

There was no pronouncement of power or glory, no threat to the Roman conquerors, no criticism of the misguided rabbis or priests. Just a beautiful emphasis of his desire to be a part of our personal life by showing love, compassion and understanding for our broken hearts, for our mental and emotional hurts and bruises. He came to help the people the world calls the losers, the failures, the rejects, and outcasts. He came to give compassion and comfort to those who are hurting, those who are confused and discouraged, people who have made mistakes but want to get right with themselves and with God: "As one whom his mother comforteth, so will I comfort you." (Isaiah 66:13.)

In great tenderness Jesus said, "Blessed are they that mourn." How can we be blessed by difficulties that cause us to mourn? Let us consider the entire verse: "Blessed are they that mourn: for they shall be comforted." (Matthew 5:4.) Ask any person who has received this divine comfort from the Lord in the time of their mourning, and they will tell you that the cause of their mourning was a small price to pay for the great treasure of experiencing his compassion and comfort. "For he satisfieth the longing soul, and filleth the hungry soul with goodness." (Psalms 107:9.) One woman who discovered Christ's compassion through the pain of her divorce related:

> My time alone was a great period of spiritual growth. I had no one to turn to, no place to go, except on my knees.
>
> I prayed as I had never prayed before. I fasted faithfully, meaningfully, and often. I read and studied the scriptures from cover to cover for the first time in my life.
>
> On my knees, I experienced complete dependence upon God.
>
> And he was there. He heard my humble pleadings. He put his arm of love around me. He forgave me of my sins and showed me a better way. I was amazed at the happiness, success, and opportunity that came into my life. (Mary Jane Knights, *Ensign*, August 1985, p.50.)

One barrier preventing us from experiencing the Savior's compassion is the mistaken idea that he is so infinitely superior to us that he could never understand or care about our fears, hurts, weaknesses, discouragements, temptations, etc. But Christ's perfection in purity and holiness does not mean that he cannot understand or feel compassion for our difficulties. Because he is perfect, so is his compassion.

When Jesus came to earth to minister as our Savior, he agreed to experience mortality in all its fullness. He came not as a spectator, but as a participant. "Wherefore in all things it behoved him to be made like unto his brethren, that he might be a merciful and faithful high priest." (Hebrews 2:17.) Because "the children are partakers of flesh and blood, he also himself likewise took part of the same." (Hebrews 2:14.)

We see his desire to be perfectly compassionate in the degree to which he "likewise took part of the same." He could have chosen to view our sorrows, temptations, weaknesses and pains vicariously. He could have chosen to know them secondhand, through the power of the Holy Ghost, which "knoweth all things" and can teach all things. But because of his infinite love, because he wanted to be perfect in his ability to minister compassion and comfort in our distress, Jesus Christ chose to encounter the experiences of mortality first-hand, in the flesh, exactly as we do.

> And he shall go forth, suffering pains and afflictions and temptations of every kind; and this that the word might be fulfilled which saith he will take upon him the pains and the sicknesses of his people.
>
> And he will take upon him their infirmities, that his bowels may be filled with mercy, according to the flesh, that he may know according to the flesh how to succor his people according to their infirmities.
>
> Now the Spirit knoweth all things; nevertheless the Son of God suffereth according to the flesh that he might take upon him the sins of his people, that he might blot out their transgressions according to the power of his deliverance. (Alma 7:11-13.)

Because of this personal, firsthand exposure to the difficulties of life which bring sorrow and pain, Jesus is now able to minister unto us perfect comfort and perfect compassion. It is true that he has commanded us to conquer our imperfections and to grow toward perfect holiness. But meanwhile, because he himself has known the difficulty of our quest, his compassion for us as we struggle along the path, is perfect. "I will that ye should overcome the world; wherefore I will have compassion upon you." (D&C 64:2.)

Ezra Taft Benson states: "Indeed there is no human condition—be it suffering, incapacity, inadequacy, mental deficiency, or sin—which He cannot comprehend or for which His love will not reach out to the individual. He pleads today: 'Come unto me, all ye that labour and are heavy laden, and I will give you rest.' (Matthew 11:28.)" (Ezra Taft Benson, *Ensign*, November 1983, p.8.)

The sad part of all this is that we are so often unaware of his compassionate intervention in our lives. One day as I walked down the hall at work, I noticed a woman leaning against the wall, talking to her supervisor. As I approached, I noticed tears streaming down her face and even though I didn't know her and couldn't hear the conversation, I could see the anguish and pleading in her expression. The supervisor's face, however, was cold and unyielding. This isn't right, I thought to myself. No matter what the problem, even if he cannot grant her desire, he could at least respond with compassion rather than with cold indifference. I wanted to interrupt. I wanted to put my arm around her and say, "I am your brother and I care. I probably can't help with your problem, but I just want you to know that I care and would help if I could." Of course the political structure of management-employee relations doesn't permit such intrusions.

As I contemplated that occasion, and sorrowed that this woman went through it without comfort, I felt grateful to know that we have a Father in Heaven and a Savior who are perfectly aware of our problems and yearn to give us comfort and encouragement. I have glimpsed the infinite concern they have for us by realizing that if I, a mere mortal and stranger to this woman, can be moved so deeply with feelings of concern for her, how much more must our perfect Heavenly Father and Savior feel for each of us.

Just as this woman suffered her burden alone, unaware of my feelings of compassion for her, so we too are often unaware of the Savior's compassion for our difficulties. In fact, we are told that when the Millennium arrives and we are able to look back over the past affairs of our lives, one of the great surprises will be our discovery of just how intimately Jesus Christ was involved in our difficulties and sorrows. What love we will feel for him as we learn that he was with us in every problem and heartache, usually unseen, unnoticed, offering compassion and comfort, even carrying us when we were too weary to go on by ourselves:

"In all their afflictions he was afflicted. And the angel of his presence saved them; and in his love, and in his pity, he redeemed them, and bore them, and carried them all the days of old." (D&C 133:53.)

It is wonderful to anticipate that joyous day when the Lord will remove the presence of evil from our world and administer the perfect comfort and compassion he cannot presently provide without intruding on our probationary experiences. "And God shall wipe away all tears from their eyes; and there shall be no more death, neither sorrow, nor crying, neither shall there be any more pain: for the former things are passed away." (Revelations 21:4; See also Isaiah 25:8; Revelations 7:17.) Meanwhile, as we await that glorious day of millennial reign, let us "Look unto God with firmness of mind, and pray unto him with exceeding faith, and he will console you in your afflictions, and will plead your cause, and send down justice upon those who seek your destruction." (Jacob 3:1.)

In a sermon at a Single Adult Fireside, President Gordon B. Hinckley told how he was touched by the experience of Ginger Evans, a single parent raising seven children by herself. Weighed down by the burdens in her life, she pleaded with her Father in Heaven for the privilege of coming to him, if only for one night, to find comfort and strength for the trials to come. Tender was the answer that formed in her mind:

"You cannot come to me but I will come to you."

President Hinckley then observed, "No, we do not leave this life at our own will for a heavenly respite. God our Eternal Father would not have it so. But He and His Beloved Son can come to us by the power of the Spirit to comfort and sustain, to nurture and to bless." (*Ensign*, June 1989, p.74.) This same compassion is available to each one of us in our own difficulties, because the Savior has promised the faithful, "I will not leave you comfortless: I will come to you." (John 14:18.)

Most importantly, you need to kneel in fervent prayer to Father in Heaven and place yourself in his hands. Then put your confidence in him and say, "I've got a burden I've been carrying, and I'm tired of having it weigh me down, and I'm too tired to carry it

alone. Would you please help me?" He will. He really
will. (*New Era*, April 1990, p. 17.)

Many prophets have testified that God is "full of compassion, and gracious, longsuffering, and plenteous in
mercy and truth." (Psalms 86:15.) As we struggle to conquer our weaknesses and sins, and especially when our
level of performance falls beneath the ideal we are reaching
for, it is important to know that "The Lord is gracious, and
full of compassion, slow to anger, and of great mercy."
(Psalms 145:8.) The Lord has stated:"Verily I say unto you,
notwithstanding their sins, my bowels are filled with compassion towards them. I will not utterly cast them off; and
in the day of wrath I will remember mercy." (D&C 101:9.)

Each time we stumble, Satan is at our side, ridiculing,
belittling, shouting that because of our faults and failings
we will be "utterly cast off." Let us shun such lies by
remembering the Savior's promise that his "bowels are filled
with compassion" for us in spite of our faults.

If any people ever deserved to be "utterly cast off" it was
the ancient Israelites. "But he, being full of compassion, forgave their iniquity, and destroyed them not: yea, many a
time turned he his anger away, and did not stir up all his
wrath." (Psalms 78:38.) Because God never changes, that
same patience and compassion is offered to us today. "Like
as a father pitieth his children, so the Lord pitieth them
that fear him." (Psalms 103:13.) Because of the Savior's
compassion for our mistakes, his atonement makes it possible for him to take us back to our home in heaven.

Having ascended into heaven, having the bowels
of mercy; being filled with compassion towards the
children of men; standing betwixt them and justice;
having broken the bands of death, taken upon himself their iniquity and their transgressions, having
redeemed them, and satisfied the demands of justice. (Mosiah 15:9.)

The Arms of Patience

As the scriptures describe the arms of our Savior's love, they also portray them as arms of patience and longsuffering with us in our weaknesses and sins. "Notwithstanding I shall lengthen out mine arm unto them from day to day," the Savior said, "they will deny me; nevertheless, I will be merciful unto them . . . if they will repent and come unto me; for mine arm is lengthened out all the day long, saith the Lord God of Hosts." (2 Nephi 28:32.)

I once observed something at church that disturbed me greatly. One of the young children in the congregation was making a disturbance. Unable to quiet the child, the angry and impatient mother yanked the child off the bench and literally dragged him down the aisle as he screamed in fear of the coming punishment. This event saddened me because there have been times when I felt similar impatience with my own children, being more concerned about my embarrassment and inconvenience than I was for their tender feelings.

At the grocery store I observed a young child reach for an enticing, brightly colored package on one of the shelves. With impatience the mother slapped him and said "I told you not to touch things!" How grateful I am to know that Jesus Christ is not a God of impatience. The Lord never strikes out in a moment of uncontrolled frustration because "He doeth not anything save it be for the benefit of the world; for he loveth the world, even that he layeth down his own life that he may draw all men unto him." (2 Nephi 26:24.) As a God of perfection, The Savior's patience is also perfect. "But to Israel he saith, All day long I have stretched forth my hands unto a disobedient and gainsaying people." (Romans 10:21.)

Indeed, so characteristic is this kind attribute of our Savior that Paul described him as "the God of patience." (Romans 15:5.) David proclaimed, "Thou . . . art a God full of compassion, and gracious, longsuffering, and plenteous in mercy and truth." (Psalms 86:15.) And Moses taught his people that "The Lord God [is] merciful and gracious, longsuffering and abundant in goodness and truth." (Exodus 34:6.) As Alma taught his people what Jesus would be like when he came into mortality, he also emphasized the Savior's perfect patience:

> And not many days hence the Son of God shall come in his glory; and his glory shall be the glory of the Only Begotten of the Father, full of grace, equity, and truth, full of patience, mercy, and long-suffering, quick to hear the cries of his people and to answer their prayers. (Alma 9:26.)

During his mortal ministry, the Savior demonstrated that his infinite, perfect patience is active, not passive. Patiently he endured every injustice and insult that ignorant and conspiring men cast upon him. "Wherefore they scourge him, and he suffereth it; and they smite him, and he suffereth it. Yea, they spit upon him, and he suffereth it, because of his loving kindness and his long-suffering towards the children of men." (1 Nephi 19:9.)

And now, having perfect patience through the bitter trials of his mortal life, he continues to extend the same loving patience to us today as we stumble and grope our way through the sinfulness of mortality. "And how merciful is our God unto us, for he remembereth the house of Israel . . . and he stretches forth his hands unto them all the day long; and they are a stiffnecked and a gainsaying people; but as many as will not harden their hearts shall be saved in the kingdom of God." (Jacob 6:4.)

The Psalmist writes, "For their heart was not right with him, neither were they stedfast in his covenant. But he, being full of compassion, forgave their iniquity, and destroyed them not; yea, many a time turned he his anger away, and did not stir up all his wrath. For he remembered that they were but flesh." (Psalms 78:37-39.)

Orson F. Whitney told of the conversion of an elite lady of substantial social standing. Thrilled with the concepts of salvation for the dead and being able to be sealed to her deceased husband, she vowed to be baptized, if need be, even "in a lake of living fire." The baptism was arranged, but she did not come. Instead she sent a pitiful note of apology:

> I never knew till now what a poor, weak, frail creature I am. I thought myself brave enough to take this step; but I am not. If I should become a "Mormon" all my friends would forsake me, I would lose my social standing, and my name would be cast out as evil. I cannot make the sacrifice. And yet I believe the doctrine true, and that you are a real servant of God. I hope the time will come when we can stand upon the same plane and be brother and sister in the Church of Christ; but I cannot do that now. (*Exceptional Stories From the Lives of Our Apostles*, Salt Lake City, Utah: Deseret Book, 1972, p.275.)

I wept as I read her words. Her retreat was so like my own. Her wavering reminded me of the many times I had chosen and really intended to obey a particular commandment and then backed out when temptations came, and said, in my weakness: "I just cannot make that sacrifice now. It is too hard for me to obey. I am too weak and frail and I find too much pleasure in this sin. I really want to obey and someday I will gain the strength to resist." I wept because I knew, by the guilt from my own vacillations, something of the sorrow she must have suffered in consequence of her tragic cowardice. Elder Whitney described the feelings he had after reading her note:

> It was with mixed feelings of sorrow and pity that I perused this communication. How like the

impetuous Apostle, I thought—he who said to the Master: "Though I should die with thee, yet will I not deny thee." But he thrice denied that he knew the Holy One by whom he had vowed to stand.

And this good woman—for she was a good woman, a child of Israel, no doubt, else why did she believe?—supposed herself willing to be baptized "in a lake of living fire." But when the test came she was found wanting. Let us hope that like the penitent Peter, who so nobly redeemed himself, she may yet turn and make amends . . . . (*Exceptional Stories From the Lives of Our Apostles*, Salt Lake City, Utah: Deseret Book, 1972, p.275.)

As I read and pondered these comments, with tears for her and for myself streaming down my face, I felt the powerful presence of the Holy Spirit. It seemed as if I felt the Savior's hand upon my shoulder and I heard him say, "Don't condemn yourself so. I understand that while the spirit is often willing and anxious to choose and live righteously, it is often pulled back by the weaknesses, habits and demands of the flesh. And I can accept that as long as the spirit keeps trying and coming back again and again until it conquers the flesh."

He then drew my thoughts to Peter and showed me that even he, who was chosen for that most crucial role of first President of the Church in Christ's absence, even he was subject to fear, vacillation, and double mindedness and denied the Savior three times—on the very first night. The Spirit whispered to me, "You must remember that Christ knew Peter's weakness when he chose him, but he could accept it because he had the patience to wait while Peter, through that forgivable weakness, would be made strong."

I came away from this experience realizing that while our vows are sacred and of course we are expected to honor them with obedience and devotion, and while our mortal wavering and disobedience hurts and disappoints the Lord, when we abandon our follies and turn back to the Savior, we will find that he has been there all the time, waiting patiently for the moment we choose him instead of our sins.

It is true that the Lord has commanded us to seek perfection in our daily discipleship. But he is not demanding the attainment of that perfection before he will love or bless us. Paul admonished us to "run with patience the race that is set before us, looking unto Jesus the author and finisher of our faith." (Hebrews 12:1-2.) In our own time, Jesus, himself, has commanded, "Do not run faster or labor more than you have strength and means." (D&C 10:4.)

As we do the best we can in each area of our lives, we are, he said, to "continue in patience until ye are perfected." (D&C 67:13.) So if God does not reject nor condemn us for having unconquered weaknesses as we work out our salvation, if he is willing to wait patiently for our growth toward the ideals, what right do we have to condemn or despise ourselves while we are in the process of learning to overcome them?

We can learn to appreciate the arms of our Savior's patience by remembering always that "If it had not been for his matchless power, and his mercy, and his long-suffering towards us, we should unavoidably have been cut off from the face of the earth long before this period of time, and perhaps been consigned to a state of endless misery and woe." (Alma 9:11.)

Let us never be guilty of the Savior's lament when he said, "How oft have I called upon you by the mouth of my servants, and by the ministering of angels, and by mine own voice . . . and by the voice of mercy all the day long . . . and would have saved you with an everlasting salvation, but ye would not!" (D&C 43:25.) Rather, let us resolve to apply King Benjamin's admonition: "I would that ye should remember, and always retain in remembrance, the greatness of God, and your own nothingness, and his goodness and long-suffering towards you, unworthy creatures, and humble yourselves even in the depths of humility." (Mosiah 4:11.)

There is great comfort from D&C 46:9, which gives the assurance that the gifts and blessings of the gospel are "given for the benefit of those who love me and keep all my commandments, and him that seeketh so to do." In his infinite patience, what is most important to the Savior is not how perfect we are at this precise moment, but the direction of our growth and where the desires of our heart are focused. "The Lord . . . is longsuffering to us-ward, not willing that any should perish, but that all should come to repentance." (2 Peter 3:9.)

Remembering and treasuring our knowledge of the Lord's patience is the principle of motivation which increases our devotion and desire to respond to his arms of love and patience. Alma mentioned this principle to his wayward son, Corianton, as he sought to bring him to repentance. "O, my son, I desire that ye . . . do not endeavor to excuse yourself in the least point because of your sins, by denying the justice of God; but do you let the justice of God, and his mercy, and his long-suffering have full sway in your heart; and let it bring you down to the dust in humility." (Alma 42:30.)

It is a daily challenge to see if Christ's patience has "had full sway" in our own hearts. How could we possibly contemplate the perfect, infinitely merciful, forgiving arms of his patience and not yearn with our whole souls, to respond with love and obedience? For it is the knowledge of "his goodness and forbearance and long-suffering . . . that . . . leadeth [us] to repentance." (Romans 2:4.)

We will praise our God forever. Behold, who can glory too much in the Lord? Yea, who can say too much of his great power, and of his mercy, and of his long-suffering towards the children of men? (Alma 26:16.)

The Arms of Invitation

Perhaps the Savior's most tender invitation was given when he said with such great love, "Come unto me, all ye that labour and are heavy laden, and I will give you rest." (Matthew 11:28.) However, this is more than an invitation. It is also an explanation of the truth that if we are struggling to overcome imperfections, if we are troubled with heavy burdens, we *must* come to Christ to receive peace and rest. We may, because of our inadequacies, feel poorly qualified to accept Christ's invitation, but he said, "Blessed are the poor in spirit who come unto me, for theirs is the kingdom of heaven." (3 Nephi 12:3.) We may hesitate to come to him because of our deep hunger and thirst for spiritual refreshment, but this he welcomes, saying, "If any man thirst, let him come unto me, and drink." (John 7:37.)

Prophets through the ages have challenged us to accept Christ's invitation. Moroni closed the Book of Mormon with the exhortation to "Come unto Christ . . . Yea, come unto Christ, and be perfected in him." (Moroni 10:30, 32.) Just before delivering the sacred plates to King Benjamin, Amaleki admonished, "And now, my beloved brethren, I would that ye should come unto Christ, who is the Holy One of Israel, and partake of his salvation, and the power of his redemption. Yea, come unto him, and offer your whole souls as an offering unto him ." (Omni 1:26.) Nephi's brother, Jacob, related that the priesthood brethren of his time "labored diligently among our people, that we might persuade them to come unto Christ, and partake of the goodness of God." (Jacob 1:7.) In our own dispensation, even lay members of the Priesthood have been commanded to "invite all to come unto Christ." (D&C 20:59.)

Why is it so difficult to persuade people to accept the divine invitation to come unto the Savior's arms of love? Perhaps it is because we doubt that his invitation could actually apply to us individually.

There was a mother and father who were waiting in a dentist's office with their seven-year-old son. The young boy was excited when he found some children's books in the corner. He ran to his mother and asked her to read one to him. Coldly the mother replied, "Why, I'm not going to read you anything! You're a big boy, and you can read your own story." It was obvious how hurt the boy was when he slowly turned, put the books back on the table, sat on a chair, and soberly folded his hands.

Soon the nurse opened the door and called for the parents to come in and see the dentist. Without one word to the boy, both parents got up and went through the office doorway, leaving the frightened boy alone in the waiting room. There was not one word of assurance, such as, "We'll be right back," or, "You wait here for us." Nothing. Not one word. Frantically the boy jumped off his chair and ran to the door, crying "Daddy, Daddy, don't close the door. Please leave it open." A small comfort, to be sure, but better than being left behind closed doors. In response to this frantic plea the father simply said, "They want this closed," and shut the door in his son's face.

The young boy stood by the door for a long moment. Hesitantly, ever so lightly he touched the doorknob, as if to open it. But then, overwhelmed by his parent's cruel treatment, the boy turned, dashed out of the office and ran down the street. (Joyce Landorf, *Change Points*, Old Tappan, New Jersey: Fleming H. Revell Company, 1981, pp. 52-53.)

This story reminds me of the way Satan tries to close the doors between us and our Heavenly Father and Savior. Satan would have us believe that God is hiding behind closed doors; that he is far away in heaven and has no interest in our fears or yearnings to be close to him. But it is a lie, because "He sendeth an invitation *unto all men*, for the arms of mercy are extended towards them, and he saith: Repent, and I will receive you." (Alma 5:33.)

Another reason people find it difficult to believe the Savior's loving invitations to come to him might be because we do not understand that his arms of love can reach past any unworthiness or weakness, if we will only come to him in sincere repentance. Scripture says: "And he inviteth them all to come unto him and partake of his goodness; and he denieth none that come unto him, black and white, bond and free, male and female . . . ." (2 Nephi 26:33.)

Notice that his invitation is to every person. It matters not to the Lord if they are "black or white, bond or free." Even if we feel "black" with sin, even if we are trapped in "bondage" to bad habits or addictions we have been unable to conquer, it does not matter. When Christ evaluates our life, he is more concerned with our willingness and desires than he is with our mortal limitations. If we are willing to come to him in sincere repentance, we are still invited to "come unto him and partake of his goodness."

The need for repentance is no reason to refuse the Savior's invitations. "Ye shall repent of your sins, and come unto me with a broken heart and a contrite spirit," he commanded." (3 Nephi 12:19.) Nowhere in the scriptures do we find the Savior's invitation extended to people who need no repentance. There is no such person. "Repent all ye ends of the earth, and come unto me . . . that ye may be saved." (Moroni 7:34.) And further, "Therefore, whoso repenteth and cometh unto me as a little child, him will I receive, for of such is the kingdom of God. Behold, for such I have laid down my life, and have taken it up again; therefore repent, and come unto me ye ends of the earth, and be saved." (3 Nephi. 9:22.)

For whom did Christ die? Who is typical of the kingdom of God? Repentant sinners who exercise their faith in Christ by accepting his invitation to come to him. "Yea, verily I say unto you, if ye will come unto me ye shall have eternal life. Behold, mine arm of mercy is extended towards you, and whosoever will come, him will I receive; and blessed are those who come unto me." (3 Nephi 9:14.)

Jesus Christ is not a passive Shepherd. His arms of love are not only extended to all who will accept his invitation and come to him willingly, but also to those who are timid and afraid to come. When doubts or misconceptions prevent us from coming to Christ, *he comes to us*. To help us realize this, the Savior said, "Behold, I stand at the door, and knock:" and then he promised, "If any man hear my voice, and open the door, I will come in to him." (Revelations 3:20.)

Notice the Savior did not say, "I will only come in if the person is good enough." What he did say is that every sincere person who opens the door will receive his fellowship. Speaking of this scripture, President Ezra Taft Benson asked us to notice that "He does not say, 'I stand at the door and wait for you to knock.' He is calling, beckoning, asking that we simply open our hearts and let him in." (*Ensign*, October 1989, p. 4.) So it is not the Savior who is hiding behind closed doors, it is *us*. As a loving Shepherd, Jesus Christ is right outside the door to our hearts, knocking, pounding, pleading for us to open to the arms of his love.

Alma once challenged members of the church to project themselves forward to the day of judgment. "I say unto you, can you imagine to yourselves that ye hear the voice of the Lord, saying unto you, in that day: Come unto me ye blessed, for behold, your works have been the works of righteousness upon the face of the earth?" (Alma 5:16.) If we learn to overcome our hesitations and come to Christ in *this* life, the glorious day will come when we will "see his face with pleasure," and hear him extend to us the final invitation, "Come unto me, ye blessed, there is a place prepared for you in the mansions of my Father." (Enos 1:27.)

The Arms of Acceptance

I have always been active in the church, but for most of my life, I felt I was inferior and unworthy of the Savior's love. And indeed, because of the life I was living, I really was unworthy.

But condemned? Never!

What I did not understand was how much Christ wanted to be a part of my life and help me to overcome that unworthiness that loomed so large in my self-perceptions. I mistakenly believed that I had to somehow make myself good enough for God before he would accept me and be a part of my life.

I focused on scriptural warnings such as "I the Lord cannot look upon sin with the least degree of allowance," (D&C 1:31) and assumed they meant I was condemned in the eyes of the Lord. I ignored the Lord's beautiful assurance in the very next verse, that every person who "repents and does the commandments of the Lord shall be forgiven" and accepted (D&C 1:32.) I ignored Christ's assurance that "God sent not his Son into the world to condemn the world," and his promise that every person "that cometh to me I will in no wise cast out." (John 3:17; 6:37.)

In New Testament times nothing was as repulsive and abhorrent as the leper. Everywhere he went, he was required to call out a warning, such as "Unclean, unclean. Stand clear. Don't get too close." And that is exactly how Satan wants us to feel when we sin. "Unclean, unclean.

Don't love me, don't respect me, don't get involved in my life. Stand clear, unclean."

But Christ was not repulsed by the lepers. Without hesitation he said the same thing to them that he says to each of us today, "Come to me." And when they came, he actually reached out and touched them! That fearless touch of love and acceptance amazed the Jews far more than the healing did. Even though we are all spiritual lepers to some degree, the scriptures teach that there is no filthiness too repulsive to separate us from the healing touch of his love, if we will only reach out and accept it.

One thing about Jesus that drove the Scribes and Pharisees to constant murmuring was the fact that "This man receiveth sinners, and eateth with them." (Luke 15:2.) Christ's oft repeated reply was that "The Son of man is come to seek and to save that which was lost," and that "joy shall be in heaven over one sinner that repenteth, more than over ninety and nine just persons, which need no repentance." (Luke 19:10; 15:7.)

Even the woman taken in the very act of adultery was not condemned by the Savior. Dragged before him and thrown at his feet, the accusers demanded his judgment. If Christ were not a God of love, forgiveness and acceptance, we might have expected him to join in the condemnation. "So, you've filthied yourself with the greatest sin there is next to murder! How in the world did you ever fall to this level? Are you sorry? Have you learned your lesson?"

But those were not his words. Instead of confronting the woman or shaming her in the presence of others, he turned to her self-righteous accusers. "He that is without sin among you, let him cast a stone at her," he challenged protectively. "And they which heard it, being convicted by their own conscience, went out one by one." When they were alone, with tender compassion and arms of acceptance, he said to her, "Woman, where are those thine accusers? hath no man condemned thee? She said, No man, Lord. And Jesus said unto her, Neither do I condemn thee: go, and sin no more." (John 8:7-11.)

His concern was not for the woman's sin, but for her soul. In our own time the Savior has repeated the same assurance. "Thou art not excusable in thy transgressions;

nevertheless, go thy way and sin no more." (D&C 24:2.) "Behold, I do not condemn you; go your ways and sin no more; perform with soberness the work which I have commanded you." (D&C 6:35.)

So, come unto Christ and what is the promise? "I will not condemn you. I will not reject you. I will not turn you away." What an encouragement to know that Jesus came to help those whom the world labels as the losers, the failures, the sinners, the rejects and outcasts. He came to help those who are hurting, people who are confused and discouraged; people who have made mistakes but want to get right with themselves and with God. His gospel was not given for perfect people, but for sinners, for people with weaknesses and flaws.

How the Savior longs to wrap us in the accepting arms of his love and remove every obstacle that prevents us from returning to our Heavenly Father. How he longs to assure us that there is hope; that we are not condemned simply because we have unconquered weaknesses; that he is not judging us on the degree of perfection we have presently attained, but on where our hearts lie, where our priorities lie, on the measure of our devotion to him. How great is his desire to convince each of us that we are important and precious to him.

"Some of you are guilty before me," Christ has said, "but I will be merciful unto your weaknesses." (D&C 38:14.) And, "Notwithstanding their sins, my bowels are filled with compassion towards them. I will not utterly cast them off; and in the day of wrath I will remember mercy." (D&C 101:9.)

> Great and marvelous are thy works, O Lord God Almighty . . . and, because thou art merciful, thou wilt not suffer those who come unto thee that they shall perish. (1 Nephi 1:14.)

Nephi felt that the message of Christ's willingness to accept every person who will come to him was so important that he testified of this kindness six times in one chapter. When we consider the difficulty that Nephi had in laboriously inscribing one word at a time on the golden plates, we realize he must have felt this message was extremely important. He began by explaining that because of Christ's great love for his brothers and sisters, he "doeth not anything save it be for the benefit of the world; for he loveth the world, even that he layeth down his own life that he may draw all men unto him. Wherefore, he commandeth none that they shall not partake of his salvation." (2 Nephi 26:24.)

Not satisfied that we would believe Jesus actually wants to "draw all men" to him, in spite of their weaknesses and imperfections, Nephi immediately reworded the promise in the very next verse: "Behold, doth he cry unto any, saying: Depart from me? Behold, I say unto you, Nay; but he saith: Come unto me all ye ends of the earth." (2 Nephi 26:25.)

Still not satisfied that sinners would believe these promises apply to them, Nephi next spoke of those who desire to pray and attend church but feel unworthy because of their imperfections. "Behold, hath he commanded any that they should depart out of the synagogues, or out of the houses of worship? Behold, I say unto you, Nay." (2 Nephi 26:26.)

One person who was guilty of serious moral transgressions said, "At first I felt I didn't have a right to go to church." But then, as she learned of the Savior's arms of acceptance, she said, "But who has more right to be in church than a sinner who is trying to come back?" (*Ensign*, September 1985, p. 41.)

But what of those disciples who dare to attend church services but still feel left out and unacceptable because of their imperfections? To these repenting people Nephi said, "Hath he commanded any that they should not partake of his salvation? Behold I say unto you, Nay; but he hath given it free for all men." (2 Nephi 26:27.) Still concerned about those with doubts, Nephi immediately rephrased the promise in the very next verse: "Behold, hath the Lord commanded any that they should not partake of his goodness? Behold I say unto you, Nay; but all men are privileged the one like unto the other, and none are forbidden." (2 Nephi 26:28.)

What powerful testimonies that every person is invited and welcome to come into the accepting arms of Christ's love! Nephi concluded the chapter with this overwhelmingly convincing testimony: "And he inviteth them all to come unto him and partake of his goodness; and he denieth none that come unto him, black and white, bond and free, male and female." (2 Nephi 26:33.)

To illustrate the merciful acceptance Christ has in spite of our weaknesses and flaws, the Savior said, "Let my servant Newel K. Whitney be ashamed . . . of all his littleness of soul before me." (D&C 117:11.) This may appear to be a crushing, embarrassing denunciation to be received publicly through the prophet. But notice that in spite of the correction, Newel was still considered "my servant." The rest of the verse demonstrates that there is no condemnation in the eyes of the Lord when we are striving to overcome our weaknesses. "Let my servant Newel K. Whitney be ashamed of . . . all his littleness of soul before me, saith the Lord, and come . . . and be a Bishop unto my people, saith the Lord. (D&C 117:11.)

Let us consider another example. Martin Harris wanted desperately to be one of the three witnesses of the Book of Mormon plates. Martin was a man with a good heart, but many imperfections, including pride and stubborn self-will. Thus the Lord warned: "Behold, I say unto him, he exalts himself and does not humble himself sufficiently before me; but if he will bow down before me, and humble himself in mighty prayer and faith, in the sincerity of his heart, then will I grant unto him a view of the things which he desires to see." (D&C 5:24.)

Notice the important word "but." Christ is always a God of alternatives. No, Martin was not yet worthy of such a sacred privilege, but he was not condemned and if he repents, he will become acceptable. This revelation is not recorded in the Doctrine and Covenants just to tell us about Martin Harris. It is there to teach us about Christ's message of hope and forgiveness and that no one who loves the Lord and strives to obey him will be condemned or turned away.

Satan does not want us to believe these promises about the Savior's arms of acceptance. When a person resolves to accept the invitation to draw closer to the Savior and Heavenly Father, Satan invades and bombards the person with doubts. "Oh, perhaps the promises are true for the apostles and prophets," he whispers, "but not for the average member." "Perhaps they are true for those who are near perfection, but for you? No way!" And then he floods our minds with memories of past mistakes and present imperfections in an effort to discourage us. Many people have been victimized by such whisperings. With tears of sincerity they have expressed their self-abhorrent feelings:

"I feel lower than slime."

"I sincerely feel that I am not worth salvaging."

"I feel like I am dirtying the chapel when I go to church."

"After what I have done, I have no right to ask anyone for help, especially God."

This is wrong! No matter what kind of mistakes a person has made, no disciple of Christ should have these kinds of self-condemning feelings. They come from Satan, not from the Savior who stands with his arms of acceptance open wide in invitation to us. "And ye see that I have commanded that none of you should go away, but rather have commanded that ye should come unto me." (3 Nephi 18:25.)

Christ's purpose is not to put us down or condemn us for our weaknesses but to strengthen and encourage us, to heal us of our infirmities and sorrows, to lift us to his level of perfection and joy. This he can do and this he will do if we will only permit it. The arms of his acceptance will never reject or shun a person who comes to him in sincerity. What confidence this knowledge should give us. Because Jesus understands our weaknesses, he has offered to temper his justice with mercy and patience and "is kind [even] unto the unthankful and to the evil." (Luke 6:35.)

Our value to the Savior is priceless. He left his throne of glory to suffer and die for us, so what right do we have to judge or condemn ourselves as unworthy? His love and forgiveness are bigger than any fault of which we are repentant. With all the love of a tender and affectionate parent, Christ is concerned less with the mistakes we have made than with having things made right with him and with how we want to live from now on.

In fact, when we repent of our sins, the Lord no longer looks upon us as "sinners." Yes, we *were* sinners, but now we are different because we have changed our behavior and he has changed our position before the bar of justice. When he makes us new, our past mistakes are no longer important. There is no condemnation for mistakes that we have sincerely abandoned.

Elder Theodore M. Burton, of the First Quorum of the Seventy, whose assignment it was to assist excommunicants in returning to the church, once said of his duties: "I have been asked the question, 'Isn't it depressing to have to review the sins and transgressions of people involved in such difficulties?' It would be if I were looking for sins and transgressions. But I am working with people who are repenting. These are sons and daughters of God who have made mistakes—some of them very serious. But they are *not* sinners. They *were* sinners in the past but have learned through bitter experience the heartbreak that results from disobedience to God's laws. *Now* they are no longer sinners. They are God's repentant children who want to come back to him and are striving to do so." ("Let Mercy Temper Justice," *Ensign*, November 1985, p. 64; emphasis added.)

> There is therefore now no condemnation to them which are in Christ Jesus, who walk not after the flesh, but after the Spirit. (Romans 8:1.)
> For the Lord your God is gracious and merciful, and will not turn away his face from you, if ye return unto him. (2 Chronicles 30:9.)

I will confess that I have often pondered the mystery of how a perfect God could love me just as I am, so full of imperfections, sins and weaknesses. But the Lord has taught me that his love for us is not based on how good we are, but rather, on who we are; the children of God and the brothers and sisters of the Savior.

My daughter's cat helped me learn this lesson. His name is Savario. His color is tan and his fur is smooth and fun to stroke. Like most cats, Savario decides when you may cuddle and pet him and when he prefers to be aloof, which is most of the time. But in spite of Savario's moods, I love that cat. I love to hold him and pet him and whisper to him. What I love most is when I can make him purr.

But there is one terrible flaw in this cat. Savario is a deadly predator. It seems his greatest joy in life is stalking and catching birds. Not to eat mind you. No, that might be forgivable. But Savario's intent is pure meanness. All he wants with the birds is to torture them. After wounding a bird, he allows a partial escape, just for the thrill of another chase and capture. This he continues until the bird is too weak for further attempts at survival. Then, disappointed that the game is over, Savario bats the poor bird around with his paws, hoping for more fun. When the bird finally dies, Savario compensates for his disappointment by bringing his trophy to our front door. Ripping it apart, he makes as big a mess with the feathers as he can.

It always hurts me when we find this aftermath at our front door. I feel badly for the suffering of the bird. And I wish that Savario weren't so cruel. But the amazing thing is that none of this affects my love for the cat, because when it comes time to hold him and pet him, I don't think about the bad part of him. I wouldn't want to cuddle and pet him if I thought about all the birds he has tortured. But he's just Savario; our cat; a creature that I feel good about loving.

Being able to overlook this part of Savario, and to truly love and care about him in spite of that fallen, predatory part of him, has helped me recognize that if I can do that with a mean old cat, surely God, in his perfection, can do the same for me.

God doesn't demand that we overcome every fault before he loves us, because he knows that if we need changing, discovering his love for us will lead us to change. Yes, God has very strict standards, and he "cannot look upon sin with the least degree of allowance." (D&C 1:31.) But the wonderful assurance of the scriptures is that he has infinite allowance, he has infinite tolerance, compassion and mercy, infinite patience and forgiveness for every repentant person. The arms of his acceptance are open and inviting us to come to him.

> Yea, verily I say unto you, if ye will come unto me ye shall have eternal life. Behold, mine arm of mercy is extended towards you, and whosoever will come, him will I receive. (3 Nephi 9:14.)

> Thus we may see that the Lord is merciful unto all who will, in the sincerity of their hearts, call upon his holy name.
> Yea, thus we see that the gate of heaven is open unto all, even those who will believe on the name of Jesus Christ, who is the Son of God. (Helaman 3:27-28.)

The Everlasting Arms

One thing we must understand about the arms of our Savior's love is that they are everlastingly, unceasingly reaching out to us. Moses taught "The eternal God is thy refuge, and underneath are the everlasting arms." (Deuteronomy 33:27.) No matter how disobedient we have been, no matter how steadily we have raced toward the darkness, the moment we sincerely turn toward the Lord in repentance, we will find his "everlasting arms" of love extended in welcome and eager acceptance. Indeed, one of the most wonderful things we know about Jesus Christ is that he never leaves us alone nor on our own.

Something happened in my home town about twelve years ago that still makes me angry. As Mr. and Mrs. Anthony Gebbie were taking a walk one evening, they passed a gas station and heard a baby crying. Since the station was closed and there was no one around, they were puzzled. Following the sound to the back of the station, they found a newborn infant abandoned in a 55 gallon trash barrel, the umbilical cord still attached.

We are shocked that a mother could abandon a brand new baby, that she could not want it at all. It is unthinkable. But it happened.

As adversities, misfortunes, unwanted circumstances and discouragements of all kinds come into our lives, Satan whispers the lie that we too are unwanted. "God has abandoned you," he shouts. "God has left you alone.

You are on your own. God has forgotten all about you." If
we listen to these lies, we will find ourselves echoing the
Psalmist's pitiful cry, "How long wilt thou forget me, O
Lord? Forever? How long wilt thou hide thy face from me?"
(Psalms 13:1.) Satan loves it when we express such
doubts. But the scriptures affirm that God never forgets
us, "for God is not unrighteous to forget your work and
labour of love, which ye have shewed toward his name."
(Hebrews 6:10.) We are always on his mind and in his
attention. "Underneath are the everlasting arms." To convince us of this truth, the Lord compared his loving
attention to the affairs of our life with that of a mother
who is nursing a newborn child.

> But Zion said, The Lord hath forsaken me, and
> my Lord hath forgotten me.
> Can a woman forget her sucking child, that she
> should not have compassion on the son of her
> womb? yea, they may forget, yet will I not forget
> thee. (Isaiah 49:14-15.)

> For the mountains shall depart, and the hills be
> removed; but my kindness shall not depart from
> thee, neither shall the covenant of my peace be
> removed, saith the Lord that hath mercy on thee.
> (Isaiah 54:10.)

In our times of distress and discouragement, if we
believe the Savior and trust in his assurance that "I have
loved thee with an everlasting love," we will feel his arms
around us, lifting and strengthening us. (Jeremiah 31:3.)
But if we listen to Satan's lies and doubt the Lord, we will
indeed feel forsaken, forgotten and abandoned. What a
tragedy. I know, because I believed those lies for over 30
years. I believed that because I was unworthy of his love
he was far away and had no concern for my problems. I
felt he was not dependable and that I could not trust his
promises because they didn't seem to work for me.

But the truth is that "the Lord . . . will be with thee, he
will not fail thee, neither forsake thee." (Deuteronomy 31:8.)
The Savior has promised, "What I say unto one I say unto

all, be of good cheer, little children; for I am in your midst, and I have not forsaken you." (D&C 61:36.) Christ not only refuses to forsake or abandon us, he also gives assurance that we need never fear, "for I the Lord am with you, and will stand by you." (D&C 68:6.) We are never alone unless we choose to be. "Underneath are the everlasting arms."

But what does the Lord do when he sees wickedness in our life? Does he throw up his hands in anger and frustration? Does he abandon us and look for a more perfect people? No! Never! Apostle Joseph B. Wirthlin stated: "The Lord will never forsake or abandon anyone. You may abandon him, but he will not abandon you. You never need to feel that you are alone." (*Ensign*, November 1989, p. 75.) How exciting! God does not forsake or abandon!

However, Jesus Christ loves us too much to passively ignore our errors. When we stray from the path, he simply looks for ways to "stir us up unto repentance" so that we may return to him. "Behold, the world is ripening in iniquity; and it must needs be that the children of men are stirred up unto repentance." (D&C 18:6.) The Prophet Nehemiah marveled at the Lord's refusal to abandon or forsake his people, even in the midst of outright rebellion.

> But they and our fathers dealt proudly, and hardened their necks, and hearkened not to thy commandments,
>
> And refused to obey, neither were mindful of thy wonders that thou didst among them; but hardened their necks, and in their rebellion appointed a captain to return to their bondage; but thou art a God ready to pardon, gracious and merciful, slow to anger, and of great kindness, and forsookest them not.
>
> Yea, when they had made them a molten calf, and said, This is thy God that brought thee up out of Egypt, and had wrought great provocations;
>
> Yet thou in thy manifold mercies forsookest them not . . . (Nehemiah 9:16-19.)

So we see that there is nothing we can do to cause God to stop loving us, "for he hath said, I will never leave thee, nor forsake thee." (Hebrews 13:5.) And, "The Lord will not forsake his people . . . because it hath pleased the Lord to make you his people." (1 Samuel 12:22.) Jacob gave this wonderful assurance of the Savior's everlasting arms: "And now, my beloved brethren, seeing that our merciful God has given us so great knowledge concerning these things, let us remember him, and lay aside our sins, and not hang down our heads, for we are not cast off." (2 Nephi 10:20.)

There is, however, another side to "the everlasting arms" of God's love that we must also understand, for he has warned that he will not be mocked, and when we openly, wickedly flout his commandments, he may, for teaching purposes, temporarily withdraw his Spirit from us. (2 Nephi 26:11 and D&C 1:33.) Just as he cannot save us in spite of our disobedience, so he cannot force his love upon us if we refuse to accept it. So there are times when the kindest, most loving thing he can do is to temporarily withdraw from us so that we may experience the pain and loneliness of living without him and be motivated to repent. "If you keep not my commandments," the Savior warned, "the love of the Father shall not continue with you, therefore you shall walk in darkness." (D&C 95:12.) Notice this verse does not say that God would stop loving us because we make wrong choices. That never happens.

King Benjamin explained that it is really we, rather than God, who do the withdrawing: "And now, I say unto you, my brethren, that after ye have known and have been taught all these things, if ye should transgress and go contrary to that which has been spoken, that ye do withdraw yourselves from the Spirit of the Lord, that it may have no place in you to guide you in wisdom's paths that ye may be blessed, prospered, and preserved." (Mosiah 2:36.)

Just as radio waves do not disappear or dissipate because we tune to a different station, this verse explains that God's love is always there, available when we are receptive, but when we deliberately disobey, we prevent ourselves from enjoying the feelings of his love, as if we had tuned him out. In the next verse King Benjamin explained that he was not talking about the normal imperfections which we all have, but deliberate, wicked rebellion: "I say unto you, that the man that doeth this, the same cometh out in open rebellion against God; therefore he listeth to obey the evil spirit, and becometh an enemy to all righteousness; therefore, the Lord has no place in him, for he dwelleth not in unholy temples." (Mosiah 2:37.)

But even when we deliberately withdraw from the Lord's Spirit, his everlasting arms are still there, behind the scene, waiting and hoping that we learn the needed lesson and return to him quickly. And as soon as our repentance makes it possible, he comes rushing to us, reaffirming the love that was there even during our time of disobedience.

> For a small moment have I forsaken thee; but with great mercies will I gather thee.
> In a little wrath I hid my face from thee for a moment; but with everlasting kindness will I have mercy on thee, saith the Lord thy Redeemer. (Isaiah 54:7-8.)

Nearly everyone has made mistakes that led to feelings of rejection, feelings of being unwanted, even forsaken, forgotten or abandoned. The psalmist expressed such feelings in these eloquent words:

> Why standest thou afar off, O Lord? why hidest thou thyself in times of trouble?
> Why art thou so far from helping me . . . ? O my God, I cry in the daytime, but thou hearest not; and in the night season am not silent.
> Hide not thy face far from me . . . leave me not, neither forsake me, O God of my salvation.
> Unto thee will I cry, O Lord my rock; be not silent to me. (Psalms 10:1, 22:1-2; 27:9; 28:1.)

It is important to remember that Jesus Christ understands these feelings, for he has experienced that anguish to a depth far beyond our petty discomfort. He was misunderstood, disbelieved, ridiculed, called a fool and blasphemer and finally beaten, scourged, tortured and

crucified by the very people he came to save. Yet through
all these sorrows he was sustained by the comforting
knowledge that "he that sent me is with me: the Father
hath not left me alone; for I do always those things that
please him." (John 8:29.)

Certainly Jesus deserved the constant companionship
and support of the Father, but even that blessing was
removed so that Christ could complete his atonement by
experiencing the total pain of sin and separation from
God. In the depth of his agony on the cross, after the
ridicule and mocking of evil men who didn't understand,
the one perfect being who did understand suddenly with-
drew and Christ was stunned to feel those same feelings
of abandonment that our sin puts between us and God. In
his torment, "Jesus cried with a loud voice, saying, Eloi,
Eloi, lama sabachthani? which is being interpreted, My
God, my God, why hast thou forsaken me?" (Mark 15:34;
See also Psalms 22:1; Matthew 27:45-46.) Now, at last,
the total price had been paid, and Christ could triumphantly declare, "It is finished," because he had tasted
and conquered every sin, every pain and consequence of
sin that we encounter, including the spiritual death or
separation from our Heavenly Father's presence and support. He could then bow his head in physical death and
pass peacefully into the spirit world to continue his work.

Perhaps it was the shock of the Father's temporary
withdrawal that prompted Christ to stress so frequently,
"Behold, and lo, I am with you even unto the end," and
"He that seeketh me early shall find me, and shall not be
forsaken." (D&C 105:41; 88:83.) "Lo, I am with you alway,
even unto the end of the world." (Matthew 28:20.)

It is natural to think of Christ millions of light years
from here, sitting on a throne, next to Heavenly Father.
But Jesus Christ is not a "long distance" Savior. To experience the arms of his love, the warmth of his everlasting,
ever present arms, we must learn to recognize how anxious he is to be a part of our day-to-day lives right now.
We must learn that the "everlasting arms" of his love are
ever present, reaching to show his love, ready to rescue
and lift us toward the Father. "Behold," said the Savior, "I
will go before you and be your rearward; and I will be in

your midst, and you shall not be confounded." (D&C
49:27.) "Mine eyes are upon you. I am in your midst [even
though] ye cannot see me." (D&C 38:7.) Because of his
divine power to emanate his influence throughout the universe, Christ is "not far from every one of us," even though
his physical presence may be elsewhere. (Acts 17:27.)

The Lord is nigh unto them that are of a broken
heart . . . . (Psalms 34:18.)

The Lord is nigh unto all them that call upon
him . . . . (Psalms 145:18.)

So we have learned that Satan is a liar. God never forgets
us. He never abandons or forsakes us. "I the Lord am with
you, and will stand by you," the Savior promised, and "I will
go before your face. I will be on your right hand and on your
left, and my Spirit will be in your hearts, and mine angels
round about you, to bear you up. (D&C 68:6; 84:88.)
"Underneath are the everlasting arms." (Deuteronomy 33:27.)

When we went forth into the waters of baptism
and covenanted with our Father in Heaven to serve
Him and keep His commandments, He bound
Himself also by covenant to us that He would never
desert us, never leave us to ourselves, never forget
us, that in the midst of trials and hardships, when
everything was arrayed against us, He would be
near unto us and would sustain us. (*Gospel Truth;
Discourses and Writings of President George Q.
Cannon*, sel. Jerrald L. Newquist, Vol. 1, Salt Lake
City: Zion's Book Store, 1957, p. 170.)

And behold, and lo, I am with the faithful
always. Even so. Amen. (D&C 62:9.)

The God of
I AM

One of the Savior's most important confrontations with the haughty Pharisees occurred on the temple grounds following his tender words of kindness to a woman taken in adultery. "Neither do I condemn thee: go, and sin no more," he said. (John 8:11.) No sooner had she departed and her accusers cowered away in shame than the Savior declared boldly, "I am the light of the world: he that followeth me shall not walk in darkness, but shall have the light of life." (John 8:12.)

The Jewish rulers were offended. Not only did this rebel forgive adultery, punishable by death in the Laws of Moses, but he now elevated himself to Godhood. This they could not endure. Following a tense conversation in which Christ declared himself to be the official representative of Heavenly Father, the Jews proudly proclaimed, "Abraham is *our* father." (John 8:39; emphasis added.) To this Christ responded, "If ye were Abraham's children, ye would do the works of Abraham. Ye are of your father the devil, and the lusts of your father ye will do." (John 8:39, 44.)

Angrily the Jews spat back the derogatory accusation, "Say we not well that thou art a Samaritan, and hast a devil?" Jesus replied, "Verily, verily, I say unto you, If a man keep my saying, he shall never see death." (John 8:48, 51.) To this the incredulous Pharisees said triumphantly, "Now we know that thou hast a devil. Abraham is dead, and the prophets; and thou sayest, If a man keep my sayings he shall never taste of death. Art thou greater than our father Abraham, which is dead? and the prophets are dead: whom makest thou thyself? " (John 8:52-53.)

In response to this question the Savior prepared to tell them exactly who he was. "Your father Abraham rejoiced to see my day," he declared, "and he saw it, and was glad." (John 8:56.) The confused Pharisees replied, "Thou art not yet fifty years old, and hast thou seen Abraham?" (John 8:57.) And then, with no attempt to cushion their anger, Jesus told them boldly, "Verily, verily, I say unto you, before Abraham was, I am." (John 8:58.) The implications of this supposed blasphemy were inexcusable and they took up stones to kill him.

"Before Abraham was, I am." Why did this statement provoke so much anger that they immediately attempted to stone him to death? It was because Jesus Christ, a mere mortal in their understanding, had just said, in effect, "I am the Great I AM." The Biblical footnote to this statement says, "The term I AM used here in the Greek is identical with the Septuagint usage in Exodus 3:14 which identifies Jehovah."

Let us go to Exodus and consider Christ's first revelation of himself as the God of I AM. Moses was living in the land of Midian. Forty years earlier he had fled Egypt when the Pharaoh pronounced the sentence of death upon him for killing an Egyptian taskmaster in defense of one of the Hebrew slaves. Now, after Moses spent forty years in exile, Jehovah was ready to reveal himself to Moses and give him the mission of delivering the children of Israel from Egyptian bondage.

As Moses was tending sheep near Mount Horeb, the Lord's presence appeared in a bush high on the mountain. The bush appeared to be burning, and Moses marveled that it wasn't consumed. In curiosity, he left his flocks and climbed the mountain. As Moses approached the bush, Jesus Christ, the premortal Jehovah, revealed himself, saying, "I am the God of thy father, the God of Abraham, the God of Isaac, and the God of Jacob . . . I have surely seen the affliction of my people which are in Egypt . . . and I am come down to deliver them . . . Come now therefore, and I will send thee unto Pharaoh, that thou mayest bring forth my people the children of Israel out of Egypt." (Exodus 3:6-8, 10.)

For eighty years Moses had heard the accounts of this "God of Abraham, Isaac and Jacob," and his covenants to bless their posterity. Now he met Jehovah face to face. (Moses 1:2.) But there was a problem. Moses had tried previously to persuade the Israelites that he was the one divinely appointed to deliver them out of Egypt but Israel had refused to accept him as a deliverer. (Acts 7:23-29.)

So, in response to this divine assignment, Moses expressed his lack of confidence in being able to persuade the Israelites to follow him and asked a very important question:

> And Moses said unto God, Behold, when I come unto the children of Israel, and shall say unto them, The God of your fathers hath sent me unto you; and they shall say to me, What is his name? what shall I say unto them?
> And God said unto Moses, I AM THAT I AM: and he said, Thus shalt thou say unto the children of Israel, I AM hath sent me unto you." (Exodus 3:13-14.)

Now we see why the Jews felt compelled to stone Christ, for they considered him worthy of death just for speaking the sacred name, to say nothing of actually claiming to be the God of I AM.

Through the centuries that have followed Jehovah's proclamation that we should think of him as the God of I AM, Jesus has repeatedly used these two words to describe various aspects of his character and mission. The words "I am" appear in scripture over a thousand times, and while they are not exclusively spoken by the Savior of himself, most of them are. Reviewing some of these sacred self-portraits will help us gain a greater appreciation of this great Jehovah, the God of I AM.

I AM the Great I AM. (D&C 29:1; 38:1; 39:1.)
I AM Alpha and Omega, even Jesus Christ. (D&C 63:60.)

I AM the Beginning and the End, the Almighty God.
(Moses 2:1.)
I AM the first and the last. (Isaiah. 44:6;
Revelations 1:17; D&C 110:4.)
I AM over all, and in all and through all, and search
all things. (D&C 63:59.)
I AM the same which spake, and the world was
made. (D&C 38:3.)
I AM the God of the whole earth. (3 Nephi 11:14.)
I AM your Lord and Master. (John 13:13.)
I AM your king. (Isaiah 43:15.)
I AM your lawgiver. (D&C 38:22.)
I AM the law, and the light. (3 Nephi 15:9.)
I AM Messiah. (Moses 7:53.)
I AM the Savior of the world. (D&C 43:34.)
I AM their Redeemer. (Mosiah 26:26.)
I AM the resurrection, and the life. (John 11:25.)
I AM the true vine. (John 15:1.)
I AM the bread of life. (John 6:35.)
I AM the Spirit of truth. (D&C 93:26.)
I AM the way, the truth, and the life. (John 14:6.)
I AM the good shepherd. (John 10:11; D&C 50:44.)
I AM the door of the sheep. (John 10:7.)
I AM come that they might have life. (John 10:10.)
I AM Jesus Christ the Son of God. (3 Nephi 9:15.)
I AM the Only Begotten of the Father. (Moses 5:9.)
I AM he who was prepared from the foundation of
the world. (Ether 3:14.)
I AM not of the world. (John 17:14.)
I AM from above. (John 8:23; D&C 63:59.)
I AM not come of myself. (John 7:28.)
I AM come in my Father's name. (John 5:43.)
I AM from him. (John 7:29.)
I AM not alone. (John 16:32.)
I AM in the Father and the Father in me. (D&C
50:43.)
I AM even as the Father. (3 Nephi 28:10.)
I AM the light and the life of the world. (3 Nephi
11:11; D&C 11:28.)
I AM the true light that lighteth every man that
cometh into the world. (D&C 93:2.)

I AM the light which ye shall hold up. (3 Nephi
18:24.)
I AM meek and lowly in heart. (Matthew 11:29.)
I AM gracious. (Exodus 22:7.)
I AM merciful. (Jeremiah 3:12.)
I AM he that comforteth you. (Isaiah 51:12;
2 Nephi 8:12.)
I AM pure. (D&C 35:21.)
I AM holy. (Leviticus 11:45.)
I AM able to make you holy. (D&C 60:7.)
I AM the Lord that doth sanctify you. (Exodus
29:46.)
I AM he that blotteth out thy transgressions.
(Isaiah 43:25.)
I AM troubled because of the wickedness of the peo-
ple of the house of Israel. (3 Nephi 17:14.)
I AM come to call the sinners to repentance.
(Matthew 9:13.)
I AM he which searcheth the reigns and hearts.
(Revelations 2:23.)
I AM your advocate with the Father. (D&C 29:5;
110:4.)
I AM the same yesterday, today and forever.
(2 Nephi 29:9.)
I AM endless. (D&C 19:10.)
I AM without beginning of days or end of years.
(Moses 1:3.)
I AM he that liveth, and was dead. (Revelations
1:18.)
I AM alive for evermore. (Revelations 1:18.)
I AM able to do my own work. (2 Nephi 27:20.)
I AM a God of miracles. (2 Nephi 27:23.)
I AM more intelligent than they all. (Abraham 3:19.)
I AM with thee to deliver thee. (Jeremiah 1:8, 19.)
I AM with you to bless you and deliver you forever.
(D&C 108:8.)
I AM with you to save you, and to deliver you.
(Jeremiah 42:11.)
I AM with thee, and no man shall . . . hurt thee.
(Acts 18:10.)
I AM thy shield. (Genesis 15:1.)

I AM the same that leadeth men to all good. (Ether
4:12.)
I AM among you as he that serveth. (Luke 22:27.)
I AM with the faithful always. (D&C 62:9.)
I AM with you until I come. (D&C 34:11.)
I AM with you even unto the end. (D&C 100:12;
105:41.)
I AM near. (D&C 88:62.)
I AM in your midst. (D&C 29:5; 50:44; 61:36.)
I AM with thee, even unto the end of thy days.
(D&C 24:8.)

The one thing common to every one of these "I AM"
declarations is that they are all stated in the *present
tense*. The problem Moses faced was a people who knew
Jehovah as the God of I WAS or the God of I WILL BE. For
centuries they had treasured the knowledge that Jehovah
had been real to Abraham, Isaac and Jacob: the God of I
WAS. And they dreamed of some day in the future when
Jehovah would once again act on their behalf in fulfilment
of his past promises and covenants with the three patri-
archs: the God of I WILL BE.

The Lord sent Moses to teach Israel (and us) to know
our Savior as the God of I AM: the God of right now. The
God who will intervene on our behalf in our *present* needs,
our *present* circumstances and situations; in our day-to-
day lives. When we focus on Christ as the God of I AM, the
God of today, we can endure whatever is required as we
wait for the glories of tomorrow.

In addition to, and more important than,
Jesus's past and future life is his eternal presence.
That is, Christ is not only Alpha *and* Omega, he is
Alpha *through* Omega—complete, abiding, perma-
nent, unchanged. As well as being before and after
us, Christ will, if we choose, be with us.

The great challenge of our lives is usually not
meditating on what we once were or wishing on
what we may yet become, but rather living in the
present moment as God would have us live.
Fortunately, Christ can be in that moment for each

of us since, "all things are present" before him
(D&C 38:2) and "Time only is measured unto men."
(Alma 40:8.)

To Moses, who was faced not with a dimming
past or a misty future nearly so much as with the
brutal presence of a godless Pharaoh, Jehovah said,
"I AM THAT I AM . . . say unto the children of
Israel, I AM . . . this is my name for ever . . ."
(Exodus 3:14-15.)

The past is to be learned from, not lived in, and
the future is to be planned for, not for us to be par-
alyzed by. God has declared himself in the present
tense. I am the Great I AM. (Jeffrey R. Holland,
Ensign, September 1974, p. 7.)

"I AM the way," Christ assured his disciples, and "No
man cometh unto the Father but by me." (John 14:6.) I
AM all powerful. I AM whatever you need me to be, to
guide you, to rescue from your bondage and strengthen
you, to cleanse and purify you, to comfort you, to perfect
you. I AM committed to do whatever it takes to bring you
back to the presence of our Father in Heaven. I AM the
God of I AM.

Howard W. Hunter, President of the Quorum of Twelve
Apostles expressed it this way: "Some of our concerns may
come in the form of temptations. Others may be difficult
decisions pertaining to education or career or money or
marriage. Whatever your burden is, you will find the
strength you need in Christ. Jesus Christ is Alpha and
Omega, literally the beginning and the end. He is with us
from the start to finish, and as such is more than a spectator in our lives." (*Devotional Speeches of The Year*, Provo,
Utah: Brigham Young University Press, 1988-89, p. 115.)

Wherefore, be of good cheer, and do not fear, for
I the Lord am with you, and will stand by you; and
ye shall bear record of me, even Jesus Christ, that I
am the Son of the living God, that I was, and that I
am, that I am to come. (D&C 68:6.)

The Shepherd of Love

I am the good shepherd, and know my sheep, and am known of mine . . . and I lay down my life for the sheep.

My sheep hear my voice, and I know them, and they follow me:

And I give unto them eternal life; and they shall never perish, neither shall any man pluck them out of my hand. (John 10:14-15, 27-28.)

The Savior has used many compelling examples to illustrate the depth of dependency he wants us to enjoy in our relationship with him. Among these examples are the relationship of a tool to its craftsman (see Isaiah 10:15; 29:16), the relationship between the clay and the potter (see Isaiah 45:9; Rom 9:20-21), the dependency between a child and parent (see Matthew 18:3; 3 Nephi 9:22), and the vital, life-giving relationship of dependency between a branch and its vine. (John 15:1-5.) But none of these symbols convey the tenderness and rich opportunities Jesus Christ has offered in the relationship with him as our personal Shepherd.

The Lord is my shepherd; I shall not want.

He maketh me to lie down in green pastures: he leadeth me beside the still waters.

He restoreth my soul: he leadeth me in the paths of righteousness for his name's sake.

Yea, though I walk through the valley of the shadow of death, I will fear no evil; for thou art with me; thy rod and thy staff they comfort me.

Thou preparest a table before me in the presence of mine enemies: thou anointest my head with oil; my cup runneth over.

Surely goodness and mercy shall follow me all the days of my life: and I will dwell in the house of the Lord for ever. (Psalms 23:1-6.)

This passage of scripture provides a wonderful description of our Shepherd's attributes. However, it is not the beautiful words we must know and treasure, but the Shepherd himself. He is the one who provides for our wants. He is the one who restores our spirits when we have been hurt. He provides comfort and companionship, he protects us in the presence of our enemies, and it is he who leads us in the paths that will ultimately return us to our home with Heavenly Father forever and ever. If there is a serious lacking or unfulfilled need in our spiritual life, then there is something lacking in our relationship with the Savior. (Philippians 4:19.)

If we really intend to reach that goal of returning to our Father in Heaven, we must remember that there is only one way back and that is through Jesus Christ, our Shepherd. "I am the way," Christ declared, and "no man cometh unto the Father, but by me." (John 14:6.) The closer we are to Jesus Christ as our personal Shepherd, the more certain is our destination. We must guard against anything that puts distance between us and our Shepherd, and thinking of him as THE Shepherd does exactly that. Thinking of him as OUR Shepherd actually diminishes our relationship. After all, there is only one of him and so many of us. Of course it is true that he is THE Shepherd and that he is the Shepherd of all of us combined, but the thought that draws us closest to our Master is right there in the first line of the 23rd Psalm: "The Lord is MY Shepherd."

The word MY is but one syllable—just two letters. It is the most wonderfully intimate of all the words in the Psalm. It is personal. It is possessive.

It constantly amazes me that our Lord can head a band of sheep that's beyond number—that stretches across nations and encompasses earth, and yet never once lose sight of me.

My Shepherd knows me in every phase of my life. He knows my name. He knows my need. He knows my wants. He knew me before I was born.

The Lord is MY Shepherd. That one little word *my* moves the shepherd-sheep relationship into something deeply personal.

To claim Christ as My personal Shepherd is the supreme act of faith.

To be claimed by the Lord as His sheep is the ultimate act of grace. (Don Baker, *The Way of the Shepherd*, Portland, Oregon: Mulnomah Press, 1989, pp. 14-15.)

Satan tries to put barriers between the sheep and the Shepherd by whispering that Christ could not possibly know or care about each individual when there are so many. But that is a lie, for "God is mindful of every people, whatsoever land they may be in; yea, he numbereth his people, and his bowels of mercy are over all the earth." (Alma 26:37.) He not only numbers his people but also knows them by name and circumstance, for "he remembereth every creature of his creating." (Mosiah 27:30.)

Jesus Christ can know, remember, and care about every individual lamb because he is a God of infinity. His atonement is "infinite for all mankind." (2 Nephi 25:16; see also 2 Nephi 9:7; Alma 34:10-12.) His knowledge and understanding are infinite. (Psalms 147:5.) His mercy is infinite. (Mosiah 28:4.) His goodness toward mankind and the grace he is willing to bestow are likewise infinite. (2 Nephi 1:10; Mosiah 5:3; Helaman 12:1; Moroni 8:3.) Christ is also the God of infinity because of his numberless creations. "Worlds without number have I created," Moses was told, "And by the Son I created them, which is mine Only Begotten. For behold, there are many worlds that have passed away by the word of my power. And there are many that now stand, and innumerable are they unto man." (Moses 1:33, 35.)

We do not comprehend the scope of Christ's infinite, numberless creations until we read the conversation between Enoch and Jehovah, our premortal Shepherd, in which it is disclosed that "Were it possible that man could number the particles of the earth, yea, millions of earths like this, it would not be a beginning to the number of thy creations!" (Moses 7:30.) Such vastness is beyond our ability to grasp, but not to the God of infinity, for "He telleth the number of the stars; he calleth them all by their names." (Psalms 147:4.) Why would he number and name an infinite number of stars, planets, and individual people? "All things are numbered unto me, for they are mine and I know them." (Moses 1:35.) Need there be any greater reason? There was no room for him in the inn on the night of his birth, but there is always room for us in the heart of the Shepherd.

As mortals, we also analyze things in terms of numbers. We count the number in attendance at church meetings. We know exactly how many missionaries we have in service and how many converts they produce each year. Our news reports are filled with numbers. When a plane crashes or an earthquake strikes, we want to know how the number of fatalities and injuries compares to previous disasters. While we should be thrilled with each convert and sorrowful for the death or injury of even one person, we are still impressed by large numbers.

But while Jesus Christ is the God of infinity, he has never indicated that he is impressed with large numbers. As far as I have been able to learn, the most important number to our great Shepherd is "one." That is the way each person is born as a spirit. That is the way each person is born into mortality. That is the way each person is saved and transformed from a fallen, unworthy person into the image and likeness of the Savior—one at a time. Yes, it is true that Christ's atonement is infinite, and reaches to all of Father's children who will accept it and make it theirs by repentance and obedience. But while his sacrifice may save *all* of mankind, it will only save *each* of mankind, *one at a time*. No number is more important to our Shepherd and Heavenly Father than each *one* of us. "The Lord is MY Shepherd."

Jesus Christ is an aggressive Shepherd. "For the son of man is come to seek and to save that which was lost." (Luke 19:10.) There is nothing passive about "seeking" or "saving" those who have strayed from the flock or who have been snared by weaknesses or addictions they can't overcome by themselves. "I will both search my sheep, and seek them out" he declared. (Ezekiel 34:11.) In further assurance of his aggressive desire to care for his sheep, the Savior also said: "As a shepherd seeketh out his flock . . . that are scattered; so will I seek out my sheep, and will deliver them out of all places where they have been scattered in the cloudy and dark day." (Ezekiel 34:12.) Bruce C. Hafen has explained that our Shepherd's concern is for *every* burden and every circumstance:

> The lost sheep are not just the people who don't come to church. The lost sheep is a mother who goes down into the valley of the dark shadows to bring forth children. The lost sheep is a young person, far away from home and faced with loneliness and temptation.
>
> The lost sheep is a person who has just lost a critically needed job; a business person in financial distress; a new missionary in a foreign culture; a man just called to be a bishop; a married couple who are misunderstanding each other; a grandmother whose children are forgetting her. I am the lost sheep. You are the lost sheep. (*The Broken Heart*, Salt Lake City, Utah: Deseret Book, 1989, p. 60.)

In making the promise to care for our burdens, the Savior has portrayed himself as the type of Shepherd who is willing to leave the ninety and nine faithful sheep to go in search and rescue of the one who has strayed and is in peril. "What man of you, having an hundred sheep, if he lose one of them, doth not leave the ninety and nine in the wilderness, and go after that which is lost, until he find it?" (Luke 15:4; see also Matthew 18:11-12.) The amazing thing about our Shepherd, as a God of patience, is that he is willing to make that search in the wilderness no matter how many times we stray from the path. He never gives up!

And when that wayward sheep is found, is it driven angrily back to the flock? No! For "when he hath found it, he layeth it on his shoulders,rejoicing. And when he cometh home, he calleth together his friends and neighbors, saying unto them, Rejoice with me; for I have found my sheep which was lost." (Luke 15:5-6; see also Isaiah 40:11.) Not only will our Savior-Shepherd lead us back to the safety and welcome of the fold, but he will heal whatever spiritual wounds we suffered while out of the way. "I will seek that which was lost, and bring again that which was driven away, and will bind up that which was broken, and will strengthen that which was sick." (Ezekiel 34:16.)

Many repentant sinners feel ashamed when they return to the flock and hesitate to accept the welcoming arms of love offered by their Shepherd. It is important, therefore, to note the Savior's emphasis that not only does the Shepherd rejoice "more of that sheep, than of the ninety and nine which went not astray," but that "likewise joy shall be in heaven over one sinner that repenteth, more than over ninety and nine just persons, which need no repentance." (Matthew 18:13; Luke 15:7.) This loving concern does not mean that the Shepherd cares less about the obedient disciples who have not strayed. They are treasured for their faithfulness, but they are safe in the fold and can be nourished and guided by other helpers during the Shepherd's absence. But when it comes to rescuing a lost one, there is no delegation. This he attends to himself, even though he may reach for us through the arms of his servants, for "their arm shall be my arm . . . and they shall fight manfully for me." (D&C 35:14.)

Are you one who has been lost? Have difficult circumstances driven you from the fellowship of the flock? Are you struggling with a need you cannot fill, a weakness you cannot conquer, a hurt or emotional wound that is festering because you cannot heal it yourself? Then you are the one he is looking for. Come to the Shepherd. Accept his invitation. Accept his acceptance. He is waiting with open arms to receive you. When Satan whispers that your Shepherd does not know you, remember the words of the Shepherd himself, "I know my sheep, and they are numbered." (3 Nephi 18:31; also John 10:14; 1 Nephi 22:25.)

Isaiah declared in shocking bluntness that in spite of the Shepherd's sacrificial pain on our behalf, "All we like sheep have gone astray." (Isaiah 53:6.) Those guilty of major transgressions will readily identify with this statement, but others, who feel they have led righteous lives with no major deviations, no "straying" from the flock, will perhaps be offended by such an all inclusive accusation. "I am not guilty of deliberate, willful sin. How have I "gone astray?" they protest. Isaiah answers in the same verse: "All we like sheep have gone astray; we have turned every one to his own way." (Isaiah 53:6.) Turning to "our own way" involves a question larger than sinning or not sinning. It is the real issue in the relationship between sheep and Shepherd, between disciple and Master. It is the vanity of self-will, or in other words, the sin of trying to be our own shepherd. "They seek not the Lord to establish his righteousness, but every man walketh in his own way." (D&C 1:16.)

Many voices proclaim the exaggerated message of self-sufficiency, of "doing our own thing," of finding our own way to whatever pleases us instead of following the Shepherd. "Behold, they do not desire that the Lord their God, who hath created them, should rule and reign over them; notwithstanding his great goodness and his mercy towards them, they do set at naught his counsels, and they will not that he should be their guide." (Helaman 12:6.) As powerful as our Shepherd is, he cannot keep the sheep on the true path, he cannot lead them to victory and abundance in their spiritual relationship with him and the Heavenly Father unless "they are willing to be guided in a right and proper way for their salvation." (D&C 101:63.)

Every disciple is required by the Shepherd to surrender the power of his own personal will to the care and keeping of the Shepherd's infinitely superior will. And what a joyful opportunity this is, for it is the Shepherd's will to help us achieve happiness and victory over everything that prevents us from being like him. His holy and perfect will is based upon the eternal perspectives that will exalt man and help him to obtain the perfection and fullness of joy which is possessed and enjoyed by the

Shepherd himself. How foolish the natural man is for choosing his own will over the Shepherd's.

Just as Christ sacrificed his life for us, true submission to the Shepherd means we are not only willing, but anxious to place our hearts and wills, our entire selves, upon the altar of sacrifice, without knowing yet what the Shepherd will require of us. For "the Lord requireth the heart and a willing mind." (D&C 64:34.) And how can we dare do such a thing? Because of our faith and trust that the Shepherd will never require anything that is harmful or anything that we, with his help, cannot do. And also because we know that when we surrender to the Lord all that we are and have, he in turn commits to us all that he is and all that he can do, so that eventually, through his great power and grace, we will inherit with him all there is in celestial perfection and glory. "And when the chief Shepherd shall appear, ye shall receive a crown of glory that fadeth not away." (1 Peter 5:4.)

Let us remember that it is not the place of the sheep to choose their own path or pasture. For this we are to depend upon the Shepherd. Our heart's prayer as we seek to follow the Shepherd should be: "Lead me, O Lord, in thy righteousness. Lead me in thy truth, and teach me: for thou art the God of my salvation; on thee do I wait all the day. Teach me thy way, O Lord, and lead me in a plain path. Thou art my rock and my fortress; therefore . . . lead me, and guide me." (Psalms 5:8; 25:5; 27:11; 31:3.) And his reply to this submissive prayer is "Be of good cheer, for I will lead you along." (D&C 78:18.) Think of it; the God of infinity, the creator of the universe, the Savior of mankind will take the time to "lead you along." "Thus saith the Lord, thy Redeemer, the Holy One of Israel; I am the Lord thy God . . . which leadeth thee by the way that thou shouldest go." (Isaiah 48:17.) So dedicated is the Savior to leading us through the perils and heartaches of mortality, that if we do our part to "feast upon the words of Christ," they will actually "tell you all things what ye should do." (2 Nephi 32:3.)

Satan has many wolves who follow the flock, seeking to separate us from the security and safety of the Shepherd's presence. But our Shepherd's promise is, "He that is faith-

ful, the same shall be kept and blessed with much fruit."
(D&C 52:34.) This does not mean he will keep us from
temptation, adversity, sickness or other afflictions. No disciple is promised immunity from these parts of mortality
which are designed by a benevolent Father to teach us the
contrast between good and evil, pleasure and pain, sorrow
and true joy. As part of the tests of mortality, we are all
required to pass through "the mists of darkness." But the
true sheep do not fear this, for "though I walk through the
valley of the shadow of death, I will fear no evil: for thou
art with me." (Psalms 23:4.) So the promise of the
Shepherd is to always be with his sheep and "keep" us
his, no matter what happens to us. "I will lead them
whithersoever I will, and no power shall stay my hand."
(D&C 38:33.)

> In his dream of the tree of life, Lehi found himself
> in a dark and dreary wasteland and saw others sur-
> rounded by a great mist of darkness.
> Holding fast to this rod in the mists of darkness,
> we, as did Lehi, grope and move our way homeward.
> As we do, we are likely to find that the cold rod of
> iron will begin to feel in our hands as the warm, firm,
> loving hand of him who literally pulls us along the
> way.
> We find that hand strong enough to rescue us,
> warm enough to assure us that home is not far
> away; and we summon our deepest resources to
> reciprocate, until we are again "at one" in the arms of
> the Lord. (Bruce C. Hafen, *Ensign*, April 1990, p. 13.)

The Eyes of His Love

Our granddaughter, Karina, entered this world of mortality with a normal, healthy birth. There was not the slightest clue of a problem. The nurses and doctors finished their work and left the baby with her mother and father in the recovery room. Our daughter, Janae, and her husband Jeff spent the first couple of hours holding Karina and marveling over the miracle of this first little child sent to them by a loving Heavenly Father. Then they let the nurse put her in the nursery while Jeff went to call all the relatives.

However, during the third call, Jeff suddenly felt impressed to leave the phone and hurry back to Karina. Not knowing why, he ended the call and rushed to the nursery. Everything seemed normal, but a few moments after he arrived Karina stopped breathing and turned blue. Hastily the doctors were called and Karina was revived. But it was not long before she stopped breathing and had to be revived again. There was no clue to what the problem might be so it was necessary to watch Karina every moment. They rushed her into the intensive care unit where marvelous machines could monitor every life sign and sound the alarm the instant her breathing stopped or even slowed.

Later that night the alarm did sound and Karina's life was again preserved. After this third episode she was given a priesthood blessing and placed on a respirator to assist and steady her breathing. Within a few days she was able to breathe on her own and has functioned normally ever since, to the great relief of all who love her.

As I have studied the scriptures, I have come to realize that every one of us is in "intensive care" when it comes to the attention the Lord gives to our "life signs." Indeed, I would not be surprised to find that there are celestial "alarms" that sound the warning when we face spiritual perils. A major theme in the scriptures is this constant watchfulness of the eyes of his love. For example, attempting to persuade a Lamanite king that the "Great Spirit" he worshiped not only "created all things which are in heaven and in the earth," but also maintains a constant, watchful care over his children, the great missionary, Ammon, told King Lamoni, "The heavens is a place where God dwells and all his holy angels." (Alma 18:30.) "And king Lamoni said: Is it above the earth? And Ammon said: Yea, and he looketh down upon all the children of men; and he knows all the thoughts and intents of the heart." (Alma 18:31-32.)

Prophets throughout the ages have attempted to convince us of this truth. Said one, "The Lord looketh down from heaven; he beholdeth all the sons of men. From the place of his habitation he looketh upon all the inhabitants of the earth." (Psalms 33:13-14.) Said another, "Neither is there any creature that is not manifest in his sight: but all things are naked and opened unto the eyes of him with whom we have to do." (Hebrews 4:13.)

> For his eyes are upon the ways of man, and he seeth all his goings. (Job 34:21.)

It is astonishing that the God of the universe, with innumerable worlds to oversee, has the interest, much less the capacity, to watch our individual lives and monitor "the thoughts and intents of our hearts." (Alma 18:32.) Jesus once attempted to persuade us of this truth by stating that God watches the affairs of this world with such detail that not even a lowly sparrow can fall to the ground without his notice. And if that assurance was not conclusive, he went on to say that God knows so much about each individual that even "the very hairs of your head are all numbered."

(Matthew 10:29-30.) This truth is astonishing because, as human beings, we would not expect that even God could keep track of each individual, when there are over five billion people on the earth, much less attend to the falling of a sparrow, or changing the count of our hairs when one falls out. Is it any wonder that ancient scripture asks, "What is man, that thou art mindful of him? and the son of man, that thou visitest him?" (Psalms 8:4.)

> Brethren, the Lord knows each of us. Do you think for a moment that He who notes the sparrow's fall would not be mindful of our needs and our service? We simply cannot afford to attribute to the Son of God the same frailties which we find in ourselves. (President Thomas S. Monson, *Ensign*, November 1989, p. 46.)

A little girl named April went to Disneyland for the first time when she was only two-and-a-half-years old. Of course she was thrilled with everything she saw, but the highlight of the day was the chance to touch and talk to Mickey and Minnie Mouse. That night she watched the parade of floats. All the Disney characters were there: Snow White and the Seven Dwarfs, Goofy, Donald Duck, Pinocchio and all the others. Then came an enormous float with her two special friends, Mickey and Minnie, sitting way up on top. Balloons filled the air as the crowd cheered, and of course Mickey and Minnie were waving to the crowd.

In that special, magic moment, remembering how Mickey and Minnie had talked with her earlier that day, little April's eyes grew wide with wonder, and she shouted, joyfully, ecstatically, "He sees me! Mickey sees me! Minnie sees me! She's waving at me!" (Joyce Landorf, *Change Points*, Old Tappan, New Jersey: Fleming H. Revell Company, 1981, pp. 119-120.)

If only *we* could maintain that same childlike assurance of the Savior's love and attention, because he really does see us and watch over us, just as Heavenly Father does. "The eyes of the Lord are upon the righteous, and his ears are open unto their cry." (Psalms 34:15.)

Incredible as it seems to we who sleep and live our lives in cycles, the Lord's attention upon us is unceasing, for "He that keepeth Israel shall neither slumber nor sleep," and "He withdraweth not his eyes from the righteous." (Psalms 121:4; Job 36:7.)

> For the ways of man are before the eyes of the Lord, and he pondereth all his goings. (Proverbs 5:21.)

I am fond of two Old Testament scriptures, even though they have some obvious translation problems as they describe "the eyes of the Lord, which run to and fro through the whole earth." (Zechariah 4:10.) We understand, of course, that his eyes are not literally "running," but rather, are scanning, searching, and observing. The second verse tells us that one of the reasons God observes our lives so carefully is to find opportunities to reward our faithfulness. "For the eyes of the Lord run to and fro throughout the whole earth, to shew himself strong in the behalf of them whose heart is perfect toward him." (2 Chronicles 16:9.) Several times in the course of the Latter-day Restoration, Jesus Christ demonstrated the truth of this verse by singling out specific individuals and stating to them, through the Prophet, that he had known them personally and watched their service in building the kingdom.

> And now, behold, I say unto you, my servant James, I have looked upon thy works and I know thee. (D&C 39:7.)
> Behold, verily, verily, I say unto my servant Sidney, I have looked upon thee and thy works. (D&C 35:3.)

Of John C. Bennett the Savior said, "I have seen the work which he hath done, which I accept if he continue, and will crown him with blessings and great glory." (D&C 124:17.) After observing Isaac Galland's faithful service in the Church, the Savior said, "I, the Lord, love him for the work he hath done, and will forgive all his sins." (D&C 124:78.) When I read verses like these, I wonder if the Savior, looking upon *our* labors in the kingdom, could make the same statements of us. The truth of the above scriptures is illustrated in the personal diary of an early pioneer named Joseph Millet:

> One of my children came in, said that Brother Newton Hall's folks were out of bread. Had none that day. I put . . . our flour in a sack to send up to Brother Hall's. Just then Brother Hall came in. Says I, "Brother Hall, how are you out for flour?"
>
> "Brother Millett, we have none."
>
> "Well, Brother Hall, there is some in that sack. I have divided and was going to send it to you. Your children told mine that you were out."
>
> Brother Hall began to cry. Said he had tried others. Could not get any. Went to the cedars and prayed to the Lord and the Lord told him to go to Joseph Millett.
>
> "Well, Brother Hall, you needn't bring this back if the Lord sent you for it. You don't owe me for it."
>
> His journal continued: You can't tell how good it made me feel to know that the Lord knew that there was such a person as Joseph Millett. (Cited by Eugene England, *New Era*, July 1975, p. 28.)

This experience demonstrates several important truths. To begin with, we find the comforting assurance that Brother Hall's need did not go unnoticed in the heavens above, nor does ours. God saw the hungering need of his children just as he sees our needs, whatever they may be. And second, looking upon the people who lived in Brother Hall's neighborhood, he saw all those who *could* help him and then chose the one he knew *would* help. Having watched years of Joseph Millett's selfless sacrificial service in the kingdom, the Lord knew he could count on him to share in this time of need.

Having revealed to Brother Hall the place to get help, can you contemplate the joy in heaven that day as the Lord then watched the fulfillment of his confidence in Joseph Millet? And can you imagine Christ's joy as he and Heavenly Father watched Brother Hall's family gratefully partake of adequate nourishment that evening.

Now my brethren, we see that God is mindful of every people, whatsoever land they may be in; yea, he numbereth his people, and his bowels of mercy are over all the earth. (Alma 26:37.)

Brother Millet's astonishment that God knew him by name is understandable to me because I was over forty years old before I learned for myself that God truly does know and watch over every individual on this earth. As Elder Horacio A. Tenorio, of the Second Quorum of Seventy said, "Our Heavenly Father loves us dearly and watches over us in all our needs and cares, following us through life step by step." (*Ensign*, May 1990, p. 79.)

Elder Paul H. Dunn has also given testimony that "God the Father has not forgotten us here in mortality. He has not removed himself to a far corner of the universe to watch our antics with indifference." He said, "Many people believe that he's done just that. They can't believe that he could create a universe, people a world with billions of souls, and still care a whit what happens to a single individual with his small concerns. They can't believe that they're that important to anyone, let alone to the Creator of it all. May I tell you that I know that God lives, that he cares, and that he knows each one of us individually by name." (*Ensign*, May 1979, p. 8.)

As I was traveling across town one day, I noticed that the woman driving the car next to me was crying. No, not just crying, but really sobbing. For about ten miles we drove side by side, pausing at the same lights. The woman was a total stranger, but as I watched her pour out her grief, I could not help grieving for her.

What was so awful, I wondered. Could it be an unexpected financial difficulty that she didn't know how to solve? Had a loved one just died? Was it a problem with one of her children? Or perhaps because she had no children to go home to? Perhaps it was a problem in her marriage? Or loneliness from not having a husband or family? There were hundreds of possibilities.

I have learned that our sorrows hurt the most when we think we must bear them alone; that no one else knows, or cares. That tragic, unnecessary sense of aloneness is often worse than the burden itself. That is why it is so important to know about the eyes of the Savior's love. Here was a sister, a fellow child of God who was suffering alone, unaware that I had noticed her distress. Did she know that there is a loving Father in Heaven and a Savior who long to share our burdens? If only I could tell her of their love and concern.

The farther we drove and the longer her weeping persisted, the more compelled I felt to jump out of my car at one of the red lights and motion her to open her window. "You don't know me, I would say, "but I can see that you are hurting and I wanted you to know that I care. If you'll pull over at the next parking spot, I'll gladly listen to your problem. I may not be able to help, but I promise I'll listen and I'll care about you, my sister." Or could I just use the Savior's magnificently tender question, "Woman, why weepest thou?" (John 20:15.)

Unfortunately our society doesn't allow such intimacies between strangers. I recognized that were I to make such an approach, it would probably have only added to her distress, her privacy having been penetrated by a stranger she couldn't trust. So we crossed the city without communication, her heart aching from a problem I could not discern, and mine aching because I wanted to help but couldn't.

When our paths finally parted, I watched her drive on, still weeping. My sorrow for her was measurably increased by the fact that she bore her burden alone, unaware that she had a brother in the very next car who cared and was aware of her sorrow. However, I knew that Jesus Christ was aware of this woman, and I could pray that she knew or would be told about the eyes of his love, the arms of his compassion, tenderness, and love.

> Verily, verily, I say unto you that mine eyes are upon you. I am in your midst and ye cannot see me. (D&C 38:7.)

The God of "All Things"

The Prophet Joseph seldom complained about the incredible difficulty and opposition which he encountered. But after suffering many long months of cold, lonely, and unjust captivity in Liberty Jail, he finally spoke that woeful prayer of "why" that we often repeat in our own adversities. In reply, the Lord taught Joseph the principle that God has the power to bring good from every circumstance, no matter how undesirable they may seem. "My son," the Lord replied, "peace be unto thy soul; thine adversity and thine afflictions shall be but a small moment," and "know thou, my son, that all these things shall give thee experience and shall be for thy good." (D&C 121:7; 122:7.)

This principle is important to our own faith because Satan continually tries to use adversity as a wedge between us and the Lord. "How could you possibly think God loves you or cares about you when he allowed this to happen to you?" he challenges. We will not crumble before these satanic taunts if we remember that one of the important reasons we chose to come to this mortal school was to gain "experience." Our bond with the Lord will be further strengthened if we remember his sacred, unwavering promise to watch over and influence our affairs so that "all things shall work together for your good." (D&C 105:40.) The Lord is so committed to this promise that he has repeated it many times. For example, "We know that all things work together for good to them that love God, to them who are called according to his purpose." (Romans 8:28.) And again, "Let your hearts be comforted; for all things shall work together for good to them that walk uprightly." (D&C 100:15.)

Perhaps the greatest tests of this promise are the unjust adversities that afflict man even when he is trying to live in harmony with the commandments. That is why it is so important to know that Christ is a God of power, and that he delights in manifesting his power by changing our misfortunes into blessings. The way we may rise above the difficulties which turn many to bitterness and anger with God is to remember that God never leaves us alone. He actually goes through the afflictions with us so that he may convert them to our good. "Be patient in afflictions, for thou shalt have many; but endure them, for, lo, I am with thee, even unto the end of thy days." (D&C 24:8.)

By understanding the degree to which Christ is involved in the affairs of this mortal world, we realize there is absolutely nothing that is not under his control. "He is before all things, and by him all things consist." (Colossians 1:17.) And because he is involved in every circumstance that affects our progress toward exaltation, "he hath given a law unto all things, by which they move in their times and their seasons." (D&C 88:42.) To ensure that his laws are obeyed, and that nothing can happen to us which he cannot turn to our good, he has assured us that "I am over all, and in all, and through all, and search all things." (D&C 63:59.)

So total is his searching and understanding of every experience of mortality that "in all things it behoved him to be made like unto his brethren, that he might be a merciful and faithful high priest in things pertaining to God." (Hebrews 2:17.) It was for this reason, to experience every difficulty and sorrow that we may face, that "he descended below all things, [so] that he comprehended all things, that he might be in all and through all things, the light of truth." (D&C 88:6; see also 122:8.) Now that he has experienced mortality and risen to immortality and perfection, there is nothing beyond the reach of his power and influence because "he comprehendeth all things, and all things are before him, and all things are round about him; he is above all things, and in all things, and is through all things, and is round about all things." (D&C 88:41.) How could the scriptures state any plainer that Jesus Christ truly is the God of all things?

We are told that one of our joys in the Millennium will be the privilege of looking back over the events of our past by which we struggled to prepare ourselves to return to Father's presence. And we are told that one of the surprises we will have is the discovery of just how intimately Christ was involved with our sorrows, though we may not have recognized it at the time.

> And now the year of my redeemed is come; and they shall mention the loving kindness of their Lord, and all that he has bestowed upon them according to his goodness, and according to his loving kindness, forever and ever.
>
> In all their afflictions he was afflicted . . . and in his love, and in his pity, he redeemed them, and bore them, and carried them all the days of old. (D&C 133:52-53.)

Because Christ does carry and support us through our trials, even when we may not be immediately aware of it, we are told that "in nothing doth man offend God . . . save those who confess not his hand in all things." (D&C 59:21.) Let us learn to look for his hand. Let us learn to view our difficulties as the opportunities they really are, opportunities to draw closer to the Lord as we experience the power of his hand in bringing good out of all things.

> The foolish believer stares despondently at his or her circumstances. The present situation seems to the foolish to be hopeless, and the grim realities of life block every prospect of relief.
>
> But to the wise, the ultimate reality is God—not the present circumstance. The God of Gideon, who can put great armies to flight with a handful of men, is not limited by our circumstances. (Larry Richards, *When It Hurts Too Much To Wait*, Carmel, New York, Guidepost Books, 1985, p. 35.)
>
> And I will order all things for your good, as fast as ye are able to receive them. (D&C 111:11.)

The God of the Impossible

It has been proved throughout the centuries that our Savior and Heavenly Father are Gods of miracles, the Gods of impossible circumstances. "For with God nothing shall be impossible." (Luke 1:37.) Almost the last words Christ spoke before ascending into heaven and leaving his work in the hands of the Apostles was, "All power is given unto me in heaven and in earth." (Matthew 28:18.) All power! Unlimited power! Power to do the impossible!

Of all the things Jesus could have said at the time of his departure, why did he choose to speak of his power? The Savior knew that his disciples would encounter many difficult situations both in building the kingdom and in perfecting their individual characters; situations that would often surpass their limitations and which they could not resolve without his help. He wanted them (and us) to know that even though he is now in heaven, he still governs the affairs of men and that he has unlimited power with which to influence our circumstances here on earth. "And he received all power, both in heaven and on earth." (D&C 93:17.) King Benjamin challenged us to believe that Christ "has all wisdom, and all power, both in heaven and in earth" so that when we face the seemingly impossible, we will have the faith to draw upon his power. (Mosiah 4:9.)

Behold, thou hast made the heaven and the earth by thy great power and stretched out arm, and there is nothing too hard for thee. (Jeremiah 32:17.)

Jesus Christ "is able to do exceeding abundantly above all that we ask or think, according to the power that worketh in us." (Ephesians 3:20.)

The scriptures contain many interesting illustrations of Christ's power to control the elements in seemingly impossible situations. When the disciples' boat was about to break apart and sink in a ferocious storm, they cried to the Master for help and he stilled the wind with a mere three words, "Peace be still. And the wind ceased, and there was a great calm." (Mark 4:39.)

When Jehovah, the premortal Christ, led Israel out of Egypt, their destination was Mount Sinai. He could have circumvented the Red Sea and passed easily above the headwaters, so why didn't he? Realizing that his nation of slaves had escaped, Pharaoh assembled his entire army of horsemen and over 600 chariots. As they approached the unarmed camp of Israel, the people were in panic. They were trapped. There was no possible escape, no conceivable solution. At least not to the mortal mind. But Jehovah was prepared to do the unimaginable; to demonstrate that he truly does have "all power in heaven and on earth."

To the fearful, faithless Israelites, Moses said, "Fear ye not, stand still, and see the salvation of the Lord, which he will shew to you today. And Moses stretched out his hand over the sea; and the Lord caused the sea to go back by a strong east wind . . . And the children of Israel went into the midst of the sea upon dry ground: and the waters were a wall unto them on their right hand, and on their left." (Exodus 14:13, 21-22.) He parted the Red Sea to prove that we can depend upon him in any problem or need, no matter how hopeless the circumstances appear to our limited vision.

Some forty years later, as the camp of Israel approached the battle of Jericho, they were once again faced with a barrier of water. This time it was the River Jordan, a seemingly impossible river to cross, being in the season when it overflowed its banks and flowed its fastest. But such an insurmountable barrier is minuscule when one has faith in the God of the impossible, who said to Joshua: "And it shall come to pass, as soon as the soles of the feet of the priests that bear the ark of the Lord . . . shall rest in the waters of Jordan, that the waters of Jordan shall be cut off from the waters that come down from above; and they shall stand upon an heap." (Joshua 3:13.)

And so it was. As they stepped into the river the flow of water suddenly stopped. Unimaginably, impossibly, it began to pile up into a heap, no longer flowing in the channel. The priests bearing the ark passed through the river bed on dry ground and the entire body of Israel, estimated to be over two million people, crossed in safety as the waters continued accumulating in an unprecedented "heap." (See Joshua 3:11-17.)

It is important to recognize Christ's power over impossible circumstances because we so often find ourselves in the position of need. Sometimes a desperate need. Paul promised that Jesus Christ has the power to "supply all your need according to his riches in glory." (Philippians 4:19.) But when we are facing circumstances that make it appear impossible for him to keep that promise, we must expand our faith beyond the limiting circumstances that shout so loudly, "There is no way out!" The Christ who controls nature can surely control the elements of our environment when we need a seemingly impossible blessing. "He is able even to subdue all things unto himself." (Philippians 3:21.)

> And God is able to make all grace abound toward you; that ye, always having all sufficiency in all things, may abound to every good work. (2 Corinthians 9:8.)

Saddened by the death of John the Baptist, Jesus went into the wilderness for solace but was followed by a crowd of over five thousand men plus an uncounted number of women and children. Forgetting his own sorrow, he "was moved with compassion toward them, and he healed their sick." (Matthew 14:13-14.) When evening arrived the disciples asked Christ to send the people away so they might go into the villages and purchase food. Preparing to expand their minds to grasp that he was truly the God of the impossible, Jesus challenged the disciples to feed the people themselves. But that would be impossible, they protested, "we have here but five loaves, and two fishes." (Matthew 14:16-17.)

We can understand their reasoning. To all apparent reality, the circumstances made it impossible to provide for such a vast crowd. But this was precisely what Christ wanted to demonstrate, that he is never limited by the circumstances that limit our vision. "With men this is impossible; but with God all things are possible." (Matthew 19:26.) After the little food they had was blessed by the Savior, it miraculously expanded to not only feed the entire crowd but fill them to satisfaction with twelve baskets left over. (See Matthew 14:19-21.)

In this miracle, Christ started with a tiny amount of food and multiplied it to provide for the needs of thousands. We might apply this example to personal budget problems where the pencil insists there is no way to meet the bills when tithing is paid. Yet thousands have testified that they have paid their tithing and then experienced the Savior's power to multiply their remaining resources to meet their needs. The Christ who created this world and all its resources is certainly not limited to the 90% left after paying tithing. His resources are infinite. As great as the miracle of feeding the multitude is, however, it does not fully describe Christ's power over limiting circumstances. The scriptures testify of even more amazing examples.

As Jehovah sought to demonstrate that he was the God of the impossible to the Israelites and Egyptians alike, he changed into blood the water of the River Nile as well as all the water in all the containers in the entire land. (Exodus 7:19-21.) Even more amazing, he then transformed the inert, lifeless dusty sands of Egypt into living lice which infected man and beast alike. (Exodus 8:16-17.) How could he bring life out of lifeless dust? "With men it is impossible, but not with God: for with God all things are possible." (Mark 10:27.)

When the children of Israel questioned the authority of Moses and Aaron, they were challenged to place a rod, or dry stick, in the Tabernacle to represent each tribe so the Lord might demonstrate who indeed held the authority to preside in the ordinances of the priesthood. Here again we see Jehovah, the premortal Christ, demonstrate his power over the impossible, for the next morning, when Moses went into the tabernacle, eleven of the rods remained mere lifeless sticks. But Aaron's rod, representing the tribe of Levi, had not only budded, it had also brought forth blossoms and even produced a crop of almonds! (See Numbers 17:1-13.) Truly, nothing is impossible to our Savior and Heavenly Father.

As Christ entered Jerusalem for the final week of his life, riding on a colt in fulfillment of ancient prophesy, (see Zechariah 9:9) the people welcomed him as their new king, shouting praises and placing clothes and palm leaves in his path. "Blessed be the King that cometh in the name of the Lord," they shouted. (Luke 19:38.) The rulers were greatly offended. They rushed through the crowds that lined the road and demanded of Christ that he silence such blasphemous praises. In response to this command, the Savior once again declared himself to be the God of the impossible. "I tell you," he said, "if these (people) should hold their peace, the stones would immediately cry out." (Luke 19:40.)

Praises from inert, lifeless stones? Impossible. We can hardly conceive of such a thing. But "The things which are impossible with men are possible with God." (Luke 18:27.) We know that each person on the earth is a spirit child of Heavenly Father as well as the human child of a mortal parent. But the God of the impossible is not limited to this method of procreation. To the Jews who boasted of their alleged superiority because Abraham was their ancestor, Christ declared, "I say unto you, That God is able of these stones to raise up children unto Abraham." (Luke 3:8.)

When Lucifer challenged the Savior, at the end of his forty-day fast, to transform lifeless stones into bread, Christ did not deny that he had such power, but merely that he would not use that power to satisfy his hunger. (Matthew 4:3-4.) Yet later, in kindness to his mother's embarrassment at running out of beverage at the wedding she was hosting, he easily transformed the water into wine. (John 4:46.) "The things which are impossible with men are possible with God."

Jesus seemed to use every opportunity to demonstrate his power over unexpected, impossible circumstances. For example, one time when Jesus came to Capernaum the rulers demanded that he pay the customary tribute money, or temple tax. Certainly there would be no requirement for the Lord himself, whose house the temple was, to pay such a tax. But Christ agreed to pay it lest they offend the rulers. What is interesting is the unlikely, unimaginable manner in which he supplied the money. Go catch a fish, he told Peter, and take the money out of his mouth! It will be sufficient for both of us. "Notwithstanding, lest we should offend them, go thou to the sea, and cast an hook, and take up the fish that first cometh up; and when thou hast opened his mouth, thou shalt find a piece of money: that take, and give unto them for me and thee." (Matthew 17:27.)

Another example was provided when Christ visited the pool of Bethesda where a great many sick folks assembled. He could have healed any of them, but to best demonstrate his power over the seemingly impossible, the one he chose was a man who had been crippled for 38 years! (See John 5:2-9.)

The Savior healed many of blindness, but none so clearly demonstrated his power over the impossible as when he healed the man who was blind from birth. Such a feat was unthinkable, unless one realized that Jesus Christ was the same person as the great Jehovah who previously declared, "I am the Lord, the God of all flesh: is there any thing too hard for me?" (Jeremiah 32:27.) Jesus did not administer to this man in the customary manner of laying his hands upon his head. Instead, he chose a completely unexpected manner of healing that would require the faith and participation of the blind man. "He spat on the ground, and made clay of the spittle, and he anointed the eyes of the blind man with the clay, And said unto him, Go, wash in the pool of Siloam . . . He went his way therefore, and washed, and came seeing." (John 9:6-7.)

When the Savior's friend, Lazarus, grew critically ill his sisters sent messengers rushing to entreat the Savior to come and heal him. But Jesus did not go and Lazarus died. This was of no concern to the Lord because he intended to demonstrate his power by raising Lazarus from the dead. But unlike the time he restored the daughter of Jairus to life only moments after her death, Christ deliberately delayed his return so that he did not arrive until the body of Lazarus had laid in the tomb for four days.

There was a purpose to this delay. It was a common belief among the Jews that a person's spirit was allowed to linger near the burial place for three days in case there might be a miracle restoring their life. But by the fourth day, they believed, decomposition of the body had progressed so far that the spirit had departed and restoration of life was considered utterly impossible. (See *Jesus The Christ*, pp. 500-501.) Thus, by deliberately waiting until the fourth day to raise Lazarus from the dead, he demonstrated not only his power over life and death, but also that he was the God of the seemingly impossible.

> There is nothing that the Lord thy God shall take into his heart to do but what he will do it. (Abraham 3:17.)

When Abraham and Sarah "were old and well stricken in age" and when it had "ceased to be with Sarah after the manner of women," it was revealed to them that at last Sarah would give birth to the long promised son, Isaac. (Genesis 18:11.) Because of his faith in Jehovah's power to fulfill his word, Abraham "staggered not at the promise of God through unbelief; but was strong in faith, giving glory to God; And being fully persuaded that what he had promised, he was able also to perform." (Romans 4:20-21.)

Nevertheless, because Abraham was now approximately 100 years old and Sarah's womb had been "dead" for many years (Romans 4:19), they were naturally surprised by the good news. Their surprise was greeted with this important question: "Is anything too hard for the Lord?" (Genesis 18:14.) Perhaps one reason the birth was deliberately delayed is that if Isaac had been born in Abraham's youth, when the promise of an innumerable posterity was first given, there would have been no miracle, no demonstration of Jehovah's power to do the impossible.

Sometimes we feel trapped in impossible situations from which there is no apparent escape. At these times we must place our faith in the one who has "all power in heaven and earth." We must know that there is no situation from which he cannot deliver us. When King Nebuchadnezzar threatened to cast Shadrach, Meshach, and Abed-nego into the fiery furnace for refusing to worship his image of gold, they boldly declared their confidence in Jehovah to protect and deliver them from even that impossible situation. "If it be so, our God whom we serve is able to deliver us from the burning fiery furnace, and he will deliver us out of thine hand, O king. (Daniel 3:17.)

And deliver them he did, demonstrating that there is absolutely no situation possible for us to encounter from which Christ cannot deliver us, whether it be a physical, mental, emotional or spiritual problem. Indeed, "he is able also to save them to the uttermost that come unto God by him," and "he has all power to save every man that believeth on his name and bringeth forth fruit meet for repentance." (Hebrews 7:25; Alma 12:15.)

> Yea, and how is it that ye have forgotten that the Lord is able to do all things according to his will, for the children of men, if it so be that they exercise faith in him? Wherefore, let us be faithful to him. (1 Nephi 7:12.)

Our faith in Christ's power to deliver us from the impossible is often diminished by the perception that he is so far away in heaven. This chapter began with the Lord's own emphasis of the fact that all power is given unto him "in heaven and on earth." (Matthew 28:18.) It is not necessary for Christ to be present to work his miracles of impossibility. While Jesus was in Cana, a nobleman from Capernaum came to him pleading for the life of his son who was dying. Satisfied that the man was sincere and not merely seeking a sign, the Savior simply said, "Go thy way; thy son liveth." (See John 4:46-53.) As the God of the impossible, there was no need for Christ to go to the one in need. He need only speak the word. "All power is given unto me in heaven and in earth."

Christ has declared, "I am Messiah, the King of Zion, the Rock of Heaven, which is [as] broad as eternity." (Moses 7:53.) So the only thing which is impossible is for us to become involved in a problem which Christ cannot solve. "I am able to do mine own work," he declared, and "I will show unto the children of men that I am able to do mine own work." (2 Nephi 27:20-21.) Let us remember that God's answer to our prayers, God's provision for our needs, is not restrained by the limitations of our seemingly impossible circumstances.

Roadblocks to eternal progress are cast aside when resolves are made that no man needs to walk alone. It is a happy day when we come to know that with God's help nothing is impossible for us. (Marvin J. Ashton, *Ensign*, May 1979, p. 68.)

The Arms of Deliverance

Speaking of our Savior, Nephi taught that "He doeth not anything save it be for the benefit of the world; for he loveth the world, even that he layeth down his own life that he may draw all men unto him." (2 Nephi 26:24.) The Savior's arms of love are ever extended, ready to deliver us from every circumstance or opposition that would keep us from enjoying the presence of our Heavenly Father.

Jehovah, the premortal Christ, instructed Moses to "say unto the children of Israel, I am the LORD, and I will bring you out from under the burdens of the Egyptians, and I will rid you out of their bondage, and I will redeem you with a stretched out arm." (Exodus 6:6.) The book of Exodus describes the series of miraculous events by which Jehovah delivered them from captivity and demonstrated his power over the elements of this world. For the next forty years Moses reminded the forgetful people of the many miracles "which thine eyes saw, and the signs, and the wonders, and the mighty hand, and the stretched out arm, whereby the Lord thy God brought thee out." (Deuteronomy 7:19.)

The Book of Mormon describes those same arms of love and power which were "stretched out" to deliver the Nephites from the influence of their enemies. "But behold, he did deliver them because they did humble themselves before him; and because they cried mightily unto him he did deliver them out of bondage; and thus doth the Lord work with his power in all cases among the children of men, extending the arm of mercy towards them that put their trust in him." (Mosiah 29:20.) We note that his arms of deliverance are extended "in *all* cases among the children of men" when we place our trust in his power to rescue and deliver.

In New Testament times, Christ declared that one of the main purposes of his ministry is to "heal the broken-hearted," to bring "deliverance to the captives" who are held enslaved in spiritual bankruptcy by their sins, and "to set at liberty them that are bruised" by their battles with Satan and their own carnal nature. (Luke 4:18.)

Modern Israel has been assured of the same assistance. "For ye are the children of Israel, and of the seed of Abraham, and ye must be led out of bondage by power, and with a stretched-out arm." (D&C 103:17.) There are many kinds of "bondage" which the Savior's arms are "stretching out" to deliver us from today. Many sincere Latter-day Saints are in bondage to drugs, alcohol, compulsive addictions to lust, overeating, fits of temper and other behavioral weaknesses and bad habits they can't seem to conquer by themselves. Others are held captive by feelings of depression, discouragement, anger, unresolved guilt, inferiority and hopelessness that pulls them down and prevents them from enjoying the fruits of the Spirit.

Unfortunately, many people defeat themselves by attempting to conquer their imperfections with will power alone. It is natural for modern man to trust in his own skills to overcome such faults. From the time we were youngsters we proclaimed, "I want to do it myself!" Spiritually, many of us never outgrow that obsession.

Ancient Israel was constantly leaning on the arm of the flesh instead of placing their trust in Jehovah's promise to deliver them. The prophets were continually warning that trusting in their own power instead of Jehovah's would only lead to disaster. "Wo to them that go down to Egypt for help; and stay on horses, and trust in chariots, because they are many; and in horsemen, because they are very strong; but they look not unto the Holy One of Israel, neither seek the Lord!" (Isaiah 31:1.) The "Holy One of Israel" is the Lord Jesus Christ, who has invited us to come to him when we need the intervention of his arms of deliverance. When we "have our back against the wall" and just can't make it on our own, let us not "go down to Egypt." Let us come to Christ, "for behold he is mightier than all the earth," and "there is no restraint to the Lord to save by many or by few." (1 Nephi 4:1; 1 Samuel 14:6.)

The Lord already has our path of deliverance prepared if we will only get out of the way and give him the opportunity to demonstrate his power on our behalf. Christ has never said that he expects us to deliver ourselves, but he has frequently reminded us that "I am he who led the children of Israel out of the land of Egypt; and my arm is stretched out in the last days, to save my people Israel." (D&C 136:22.)

> And behold, and lo, I am with you to bless you and deliver you forever. (D&C 108:8.)

> For I am God, and mine arm is not shortened; and I will show miracles, signs, and wonders, unto all those who believe on my name. (D&C 35:8.)

When the Savior taught his disciples how to pray, one of the things they were commanded to include was a request to "deliver us from evil." (Matthew 6:13.) There are three main areas of evil we need deliverance from, and the Savior has assured us of his power over all three.

First is the evil influence of our surroundings in this mortal, fallen world. No matter how we try to isolate ourselves, we cannot escape from this world's evil influence. However, the path to victory is not in escape, but in divine deliverance. When the Savior had completed his mortal ministry, he stretched out his arms on the cross and "gave himself for our sins, that he might deliver us from this present evil world." (Galatians 1:4.)

The second area is the power of temptation. Because we live in this fallen world and are "surrounded by demons," we are all subject to the pull of evil temptations. (See Helaman 13:37.) But the Savior has promised to protect us from those evil spirits by limiting the intensity of their temptations, so that we are never subjected to an enticement above our ability, with Christ's assistance, to reject. (See 1 Corinthians 10:13; D&C 95:1.) And to further encourage us when we feel overwhelmed by the power of our temptations, we are promised that he doesn't expect us to resist all by ourselves, because "the Lord knoweth how to deliver the godly out of temptations." (2 Peter 2:9.)

> You should have been faithful; and he would have extended his arm and supported you against all the fiery darts of the adversary; and he would have been with you in every time of trouble. (D&C 3:8.)

The third area of evil from which we need deliverance is the stain of sin that comes when we have given in to temptation. It is appropriate to echo the prayer of the psalmist, asking God to "deliver me from all my transgressions." (Psalms 39:8.) Many who are held captive by compulsive addictions they have not been able to conquer feel as though they are wading endlessly in a vast swamp from which they are unable to free themselves. And thus the psalmist offered the prayer, "Deliver me out of the mire, and let me not sink: let me be delivered . . . out of the deep waters. (Psalms 69:14.) Only Christ can deliver us from stain of sin and the requirements of justice. That is why we are taught to "have faith on the Lamb of God, who taketh away the sins of the world, who is mighty to save and to cleanse from all unrighteousness." (Alma 7:14.)

George Rivera was working on his car one cold December morning when he became aware of a disturbance down the street. As he rounded the corner to investigate, he found a crowd of frenzied people staring at a tenement building engulfed in flames. Some of them were shouting and waving their arms and some were just standing there, crying helplessly. As he ran nearer he could see the reason for their terror. There were two little girls stranded on the fourth floor. He could barely see them amid the choking black clouds that surged out of the window, but he could hear their terrified screams, "Help! Help! Get us down!"

Concerned as much as if they were his own daughters,

George tried to enter the building but was driven back by the intense heat. Someone found a ladder, but it only reached the second floor. He realized something had to be done immediately, or they would die. Surprised by the sound of his own voice, he found himself shouting up at the girls, "Jump, jump! I'll catch you."

"You're crazy man," someone shouted at him. "They'll kill you if they land on you. That's a forty-foot drop! Wait for the fire truck!" Someone else warned, "You could kill them if you drop them or miss them. Don't be a fool."

But George knew there was no time to wait. The smoke was getting thicker and thicker every second. "Jump, jump!" he yelled again to the girls who were almost invisible in the swirling black smoke. Desperately he prayed, "Lord, give those girls the courage to jump. Lord, send them straight into my arms and give me the strength to catch them."

Suddenly one of the girls came hurtling down toward George. With a tremendous thud, the forty-five pound girl crashed into his outstretched arms and chest. He buckled, but held on to her as they fell to the sidewalk together. Miraculously, both George and the girl were unharmed.

George looked back for the second girl but she was lost in the smoke. He knew she could not see him because he could not see her. "Don't let me miss her," he prayed. He felt impressed to move backward a few feet. "Now you jump," he called into the black smoke. "I caught your sister. Don't be afraid."

She jumped.

The impact of her sixty pounds plummeting from forty feet sent George reeling onto the sidewalk again, but he held her firmly in his arms, breaking the dangerous fall.

Everyone in the crowd talked at once, asking "Are you all right? Are you all right?" The two girls held each other, crying with relief. At the hospital, George and the two girls were pronounced safe and without injury.

Later, looking back on the incredible rescue, George said, "I came across the verse, 'The eternal God is thy refuge and underneath are the everlasting arms.' (Deuteronomy 33:27.) It answered my question of how I could have caught those girls as they dropped from such a height, and where I got the strength and courage. Somehow I know that underneath my own arms were the arms of the everlasting God, holding me, keeping Pamela and April safe." (See *Guidepost Magazine*, September 1979, pp. 15-16.)

No matter how far we have fallen, we are never beyond the reach of the Savior's arms of deliverance. No matter how unseen, no matter how unlikely or impossible rescue may appear, his arms of deliverance have the power to save us when we place our faith in him.

In praise of the Savior's arms of deliverance, Jeremiah said, "thou hast made the heaven and the earth by thy great power and stretched out arm, and there is nothing too hard for thee." (Jeremiah 32:17.) Lucifer would have us believe that our enemies are too strong to overcome and that we are trapped beyond the reach of Christ's arms of deliverance. But Jesus has promised that if we sincerely do our best to obey, "he shall deliver you out of the hand of all your enemies." (2 Kings 17:39.)

Be not afraid of their faces: for I am with thee to deliver thee, saith the Lord. (Jeremiah 1:8.)

Therefore, dearly beloved brethren, let us cheerfully do all things that lie in our power; and then may we stand still, with the utmost assurance, to see the salvation of God, and for his arm to be revealed. (D&C 123:17.)

The Arms of Mercy

Listen to the voice of Jesus Christ, your
Redeemer, the Great I AM, whose arm of mercy
hath atoned for your sins. (D&C 29:1.)

One of the overwhelming motivations to come to Christ
is the love he offers with his arms of mercy extended
toward us. "Behold, he sendeth an invitation unto all
men, for the arms of mercy are extended towards them,
and he saith: Repent, and I will receive you." (Alma 5:33.)
The scriptures contain over six hundred such discussions
of the Savior's mercy. "The Lord is merciful and gracious,
slow to anger, and plenteous in mercy." (Psalms 103:8.)
"For he is gracious and merciful, slow to anger, and of
great kindness." (Joel 2:13.) The question before us is not
whether Christ is merciful, but whether we can bring ourselves to accept the mercy he offers.

Most of us think of mercy in terms of God accepting
our repentance. "For the Lord your God is gracious and
merciful, and will not turn away his face from you, if ye
return unto him." (2 Chronicles 30:9.) "And he is a merciful Being . . . to those who will repent and believe on his
name." (Alma 26:35.)

We also connect Christ's mercy with the forgiveness
which follows his acceptance of our repentance. "To the
Lord our God belong mercies and forgivenesses, though
we have rebelled against him." (Daniel 9:9.)

Sometimes we fail to appreciate the mercy which follows our repentance and makes forgiveness possible because, in a sense, we feel we have earned the blessing. Perhaps it is easier to appreciate the magnitude of Christ's mercy when we see it extended to those who are not yet worthy and really don't deserve such kind treatment. According to King Benjamin, this includes all of us. He said, "I would that ye should remember, and always retain in remembrance, the greatness of God, and your own nothingness," and "if ye should serve him with all your whole souls yet ye would be unprofitable servants." (Mosiah 4:11; 2:21.) Jacob, the father of the twelve tribes of Israel, did not presume upon his important patriarchal status when he prayed, but said, "I am not worthy of the least of all the mercies . . . which thou hast shewed unto thy servant." (Genesis 32:10.) It is humbling to pause and ask ourselves: "Just how many of the blessings I receive do I really deserve?"

The Prophet Nehemiah was fascinated by the Lord's unwavering mercy in spite of Israel's deliberate shunning of his efforts to love them and bless them. Speaking to the Lord, Nehemiah marveled how they "refused to obey, neither were mindful of thy wonders that thou didst among them; but hardened their necks . . . but thou art a God ready to pardon, gracious and merciful, slow to anger, and of great kindness, and forsookest them not." (Nehemiah 9:17.) Continuing to marvel, Nehemiah praised the Lord because time after time when "they did evil again before thee . . . yet when they returned, and cried unto thee, thou heardest them from heaven; and many times didst thou deliver them according to thy mercies . . . for thou art a gracious and merciful God." (Nehemiah 9:28, 31.)

The Lord has given the assurance that he is just as merciful to us in our weaknesses and our wavering as he was to ancient Israel. "Verily I say unto you, notwithstanding their sins, my bowels are filled with compassion towards them. I will not utterly cast them off; and in the day of wrath I will remember mercy." (D&C 101:9.) And, "Some of you are guilty before me, but I will be merciful unto your weakness." (D&C 38:14.) These verses are not cited to encourage laziness or mediocrity in our obedience, but to stress how eager the Lord is to help us as we move toward the perfection that will someday void the need for mercy.

> Too often, in well-meaning attempts at encouraging obedience, we stress the punishment that will eventually come to sinners, and we understate the extent of Christ's mercy. (Todd A. Britsch, *Ensign*, April 1986, p.13.)

How unfortunate it is when we allow the whisperings of Satan to discourage and lead us to assume there is no hope simply because we have made mistakes or even temporarily strayed from the gospel. Speaking of the Savior's infinite and perfect mercy, J. Reuben Clark, of the First Presidency said, "I feel that the Savior will give that punishment which is the very least that our transgressions will justify. And I believe that when it comes to making the rewards for our good conduct, he will give us the maximum that it is possible to give." (*BYU Devotional Speeches of the Year,* Provo Utah: Brigham Young University Press, 1955, p. 7.)

In the words of the Bible, because of his infinite and perfect mercy "he hath not dealt with us after our sins; nor rewarded us according to our iniquities." (Psalms 103:10.) How can this be? Why doesn't the Lord make us pay for every sin? Why is the Lord's justice tempered with mercy? Because his love is more concerned with saving and exalting us than it is with punishment. Jesus suffered and died for our sins so that we would not have to suffer the penalties once we repent and find obedience. When we repent we are encircled in the arms of mercy: "But behold, he did deliver them because they did humble themselves before him; and because they cried mightily unto him he did deliver them out of bondage; and thus doth the Lord work with his power in all cases among the children of men, extending the arm of mercy towards them that put their trust in him." (Mosiah 29:20.)

The Lord is less concerned with the mistakes we make than with what we have learned from the mistakes and with how we want to live from now on. If our hearts have chosen devotion and commitment to Christ, then the power of his merciful atonement can step between us and justice and prevent our having to pay the price which he already paid in Gethsemane and on the cross: "And now, the plan of mercy could not be brought about except an atonement should be made; therefore God himself atoneth for the sins of the world, to bring about the plan of mercy, to appease the demands of justice, that God might be a perfect, just God, and a merciful God also." (Alma 42:15.)

Let us not make the mistake of assuming that we have no part in "the plan of mercy" because we think it is only for those guilty of committing major sins. Joseph Smith prayed, "Thanks be to thy name, O Lord God of Israel, who . . . showest mercy unto thy servants who walk uprightly before thee, with all their hearts." (D&C 109:1.) Why would the Lord need to show mercy to the disciples who "walk uprightly with all their hearts?" It is because every person, no matter how godly or righteous they are, every person makes mistakes, even if they are purely unintentional. It is true that some of us need more mercy than others. That is why the Savior applies "his mercies according to the conditions of the children of men." (D&C 46:15.)

The "conditions" to which Christ's mercy is promised are very encouraging. Following are six of the "conditions" which will bring the Savior's mercy into the life of every reader:

1. Mercy is promised to all who are obedient to the commandments. "For I the Lord thy God am . . . shewing mercy unto thousands of them that love me and keep my commandments." (Deuteronomy 5:9-10.) "I, the Lord, am merciful and gracious unto those who fear me, and delight to honor those who serve me in righteousness and in truth unto the end." (D&C 76:5.)

2. Mercy is also promised to those who have not been obedient but who come to the Lord in sincere repentance. "And, because thou art merciful, thou wilt not suffer those who come unto thee that they shall perish!" (1 Nephi, 1:14.) What encouragement it should give us to know that "It is of the Lord's mercies that we are not consumed, because his compassions fail not." (Lamentations 3:22.)

The person most in need of understanding the Savior's mercy is probably one who has worked himself to exhaustion in a sincere effort to repent, but who still believes his estrangement from God is permanent and hopeless. (Bruce C. Hafen, *The Broken Heart*, Salt Lake City, Utah: Deseret Book, 1989, p.5.)

3. Mercy is promised to every person who has the humility to ask for it. Even when we find ourselves in bondage to sins or weaknesses which we cannot overcome by ourselves, we are promised mercy if we will but humble ourselves and ask for it as did "the publican [who] would not lift up so much as his eyes unto heaven, but smote upon his breast, saying, God be merciful to me a sinner." (Luke 18:13.) In addition to this example which was commended by Christ, we have the promise that "thou art merciful unto thy children when they cry unto thee." (Alma 33:8.)

To those who may have neglected prayer because of feelings of unworthiness, please know that God will show mercy to every person who calls upon him in sincere prayer. Don't be ashamed to ask for mercy. The Savior is delighted to bless us when we turn to him in sincerity, acknowledging our need for his help: "For the Lord will be merciful unto all who call on his name." (Alma 9:17.)

Thus we may see that the Lord is merciful unto all who will, in the sincerity of their hearts, call upon his holy name. (Helaman 3:27.)

4. Mercy is promised to all who put faith in Jesus Christ and his powers of redemption. "The tender mercies of the Lord are over all those whom he hath chosen, because of their faith, to make them mighty even unto the power of deliverance." (1 Nephi 1:20.) But what if our faith is weak? What if we sincerely desire to become "mighty unto the power of deliverance" from our faults and weaknesses, but we have doubts because of past failures? Not only will those with mighty faith receive his mercy, but also those who reach for that faith with sincere belief.

I would that ye should remember, that God is merciful unto all who believe on his name. (Alma 32:22.)

And he is a merciful Being . . . to those who will repent and believe on his name. (Alma 26:35.)

5. Those who would have mercy from the Lord must win it by showing mercy to those who have hurt them, because "the merciful man doeth good to his own soul: but he that is cruel troubleth his own flesh." (Proverbs 11:17.)

Blessed are the merciful: for they shall obtain mercy. (Matthew 5:7.)

With the merciful thou wilt shew thyself merciful. (2 Samuel 22:26.)

6. The final "condition" that controls the flow of Christ's mercy into our lives is gratitude. We have been admonished to "live in thanksgiving daily, for the many mercies and blessings which he doth bestow upon you." (Alma 34:38.) With the great effort the Lord has made to show mercy in every condition, is it any wonder that our Heavenly Father is angry when we are doubtful or indifferent toward his divine mercy? "Thou art angry, O Lord, with this people, because they will not understand thy mercies which thou hast bestowed upon them because of thy Son." (Alma 33:16.)

The Lord is good to all: and his tender mercies are over all his works. (Psalms 145:9.)

I will be glad and rejoice in thy mercy: for thou hast considered my trouble; thou has known my soul in adversities. (Psalms 31:7.)

The Arms of Intercession

I say unto you, if ye will come unto me ye shall have eternal life. Behold, mine arm of mercy is extended towards you, and whosoever will come, him will I receive; and blessed are those who come unto me. (3 Nephi 9:14.)

For Christ is not entered into the holy places made with hands, which are the figures of the true; but into heaven itself, now to appear in the presence of God for us. (Hebrews 9:24.)

Upon completion of his earthly ministry, a major part of the Savior's heavenly role became that of intercession on our behalf, pleading and advocating our cause to Heavenly Father as he "appears in the presence of God for us." The four principal words used in scripture to describe this activity are *intercede* or *intercession*, *advocate*, *mediate* or *mediator*, and *plead*.

To intercede is to act between two parties with a view to reconciling their differences. In our case, the reconciliation needed is between God's perfect justice which "cannot look upon sin with the least degree of allowance" (D&C 1:31) and the mercy toward us made possible by Christ's atonement and our repentance. "It is Christ that died, yea rather, that is risen again, who is even at the right hand of God, who also maketh intercession for us." (Romans 8:34.) "And thus God breaketh the bands of death, having gained

95

the victory over death; giving the Son power to make intercession for the children of men." (Mosiah 15:8.)

Wherefore he is able also to save them to the
uttermost that come unto God by him, seeing he ever
liveth to make intercession for them. (Hebrews 7:25.)

He hath poured out his soul unto death . . . and
he bare the sin of many, and made intercession for
the transgressors. (Isaiah 53:12.)

An advocate is one who pleads the cause of another
before a tribunal or judicial court. As our advocate, Jesus
Christ is pleading our cause in the courts above. "I am the
first and the last," Christ declared, "I am he who liveth, I
am he who was slain; I am your advocate with the Father."
(D&C 110:4.) And "Listen to him who is the advocate with
the Father, who is pleading your cause before him." (D&C
45:3.) In legal terms, one who pleads the cause of another
is one who argues a case or cause in a court of law, one
who entreats, implores and appeals earnestly the cause of
those he represents. This is exactly what Christ does on
our behalf. "Thus saith thy Lord, the Lord and thy God
pleadeth the cause of his people." (2 Nephi 8:22.)

"For their redeemer is mighty; he shall plead their
cause with thee," for "he hath answered the ends of
the law, and he claimeth all those who have faith in
him . . . wherefore he advocateth the cause of the
children of men. (Proverbs 23:11; Moroni 7:28.)

Sometimes we talk about how important it is to
be on the Lord's side. Perhaps we should talk more
about how important it is that the Lord is on our
side. (Bruce C. Hafen, *The Broken Heart*, Salt Lake
City, Utah: Deseret Book, 1989, p. 22.)

The Lord is on my side; I will not fear: what can
man do unto me? (Psalms 118:6.)

Finally, a *mediator* is one who negotiates between parties in order to reconcile them. There is no mediator

between God and man but the Lord Jesus Christ, "For there is one God, and one mediator between God and men, the man Christ Jesus." (1 Timothy 2:5.) Thus we are admonished to "look to the great Mediator, and hearken unto his great commandments; and be faithful unto his words, and choose eternal life, according to the will of his Holy Spirit," or he cannot mediate, plead, advocate or intercede on our behalf. (2 Nephi 2:28.) In the following revelation Jesus described the actual process he uses in mediating and interceding on our behalf:

> Listen to him who is the advocate with the Father, who is pleading your cause before him—
>
> Saying: Father, behold the sufferings and death of him who did no sin, in whom thou wast well pleased; behold the blood of thy Son which was shed, the blood of him whom thou gavest that thyself might be glorified;
>
> Wherefore, Father, spare these my brethren that believe on my name, that they may come unto me and have everlasting life. (D&C 45:3-5.)

His mortal exposure to the pains, sorrows, afflictions and sins of man is what enables Christ to be a compassionate and merciful advocate. Because he experienced the difficulties of mortality in his own flesh, he now has total understanding of our problems. (Alma 7:11-13.) President Ezra Taft Benson testified, "Because he descended below all things, he knows how to help us rise above our daily difficulties. Indeed there is no human condition—be it suffering, incapacity, inadequacy, mental deficiency, or sin—which he cannot comprehend or for which his love will not reach out to the individual." (*Ensign*, November 1983, p.8.) It is this in-depth tasting of mankind's mortal woes that enables Christ to understand and "thoroughly plead their cause." (Jeremiah 50:34.)

President Howard W. Hunter, President of the Quorum of Twelve Apostles explained it this way: "He suffered so much more than our sins. He whom Isaiah called 'the man of sorrows' (Isaiah 53:3) knows perfectly every problem through which we pass, because he chose to bear the full weight of all our troubles and our pains. Why? 'That [he] may be filled with mercy, according to the flesh, that he may know according to the flesh how to succor his people according to their infirmities.' (Alma 7:12.)" (*Devotional Speeches of The Year*, Provo, Utah: Brigham Young University Press, 1988-89, p. 115.)

> Behold, and hearken, O ye elders of my church, saith the Lord your God, even Jesus Christ, your advocate, who knoweth the weakness of man and how to succor them who are tempted. (D&C 62:1.)

> And if any man sin, we have an advocate with the Father, Jesus Christ the righteous. (1 John. 2:1.)

We all need to be cleansed of sin. Jesus Christ is ready to cleanse us as we repent, and then intercede for mercy instead of punishment. "And it shall come to pass, that whoso repenteth and is baptized in my name shall be filled; and if he endureth to the end, behold, him will I hold guiltless before my Father at that day when I shall stand to judge the world." (3 Nephi 27:16.) Elder Theodore M. Burton said, "His repayment will satisfy justice and he will make that payment for you if you will only repent. True repentance on your part, including a change in your lifestyle, will enable Jesus, in mercy, to transfer your debt to him." (*Devotional Speeches of The Year*, Provo, Utah: Brigham Young University Press, 1984-85, p. 99.)

> And it is because of thy Son that thou hast been thus merciful unto me, therefore I will cry unto thee in all mine afflictions, for in thee is my joy; for thou hast turned thy judgments away from me, because of thy Son. (Alma 33:11.)

If there is an affliction or sorrow in our lives, a burden too heavy to carry, we must realize that there is no need for which Jesus Christ will not advocate, plead, and intercede, working on our behalf in the courts above. "Look unto God with firmness of mind, and pray unto him with exceeding faith, and he will console you in your afflictions, and he will plead your cause." (Jacob 3:1.)

> For I am Christ, and in mine own name, by the virtue of the blood which I have spilt, have I pleaded before the Father for them. (D&C 38:4.)

We should also understand that in his perfect ministry as mediator, advocate and intercessor, Christ not only pleads for us above. He also pleads with us directly, that we will repent and obey, thereby making it possible for him to intercede above. "Wherefore I will yet plead with you, saith the Lord, and with your children's children will I plead." (Jeremiah 2:9.) And, "verily I say unto you, that I, the Lord, will contend with Zion, and plead with her strong ones, and chasten her until she overcomes and is clean before me." (D&C 90:36.)

Catherine Marshall had an experience which illustrates what we have been discussing. It came to her at a time in her life when she felt abandoned and isolated from God because of her feelings of inferiority and inadequacy in her efforts to fully obey the commandments. One day as she sat alone in her living room chair, pondering her status with Heavenly Father, she felt the presence of the Savior draw near.

"We are going on a journey," he said.

She soon found herself in a long room. She was aware that crowds of people lined the walls on both sides of the room. In the crowd she spotted people she knew—people who had died. There was her husband and her father, her grandson, no longer a baby, but a tall, slim, boy. And there was her granddaughter, Amy, a delightful little girl.

But there was no opportunity to rejoice in seeing loved ones because they were approaching the end of the room where God the Father stood, awaiting her arrival. As she admired the glorious robes of white worn by everyone else, she glanced down at her own clothing and discovered, to her horror, that she was dressed in rags, torn, unwashed, filthy. How could she come before Heavenly Father so unprepared? As they stopped before his throne, she could not even look up. She had never felt so unworthy.

But in that very instant of discovering her need, the Savior spread wide the robe he was wearing and completely covered her with it. "Now," he told her, "My Father does not see you at all, only Me. Not your sins, but My righteousness. I cover for you."

> I will greatly rejoice in the Lord . . . for he hath clothed me with the garments of salvation, he hath covered me with the robe of righteousness. (Isaiah 61:10.)

Suddenly Catherine found herself aware of the living room and her chair again. But now, instead of despair, she was engulfed in the feelings of joy and gratitude which washed over her, assuring her of the Savior's love and his power to intercede on her behalf because of her efforts to obey to the best of her ability. She was not yet perfect, but now she knew that it was precisely because he knows the pain of our imperfections that he is so anxious to plead for us above. (*Meeting God At Every Turn*, Carmel, New York: Guidepost Books, 1980, pp. 245-246.)

Colin B. Douglas explained,

> We (each) must be made clean, and we must also be declared not guilty of sin . . . in order to return to our Father in glory. The problem is that we have all been guilty. How can we who have been guilty be declared innocent?" His answer is important: "Only by allowing the innocence of Christ to be put in the place of our guilt; by taking upon us the name of Christ, as we witness in baptism and the sacrament, so that when the Father looks upon us it is, in one sense, as if he looks upon the Son. (*Ensign*, April 1989, p. 15.)

> But inasmuch as they will repent, thou art gracious and merciful, and wilt turn away thy wrath when thou lookest upon the face of thine Anointed. (D&C 109:53.)

The Arms of Forgiveness

Just as the Savior's arms are perpetually extended toward us in mercy, so they are extended in forgiveness for repented sins. Jesus Christ is a God who is "keeping mercy for thousands, forgiving iniquity and transgression and sin." (Exodus 34:7.) And yet many sincere people are hesitant to ask for the Lord's forgiveness. They may feel, perhaps subconsciously, that God is reluctant to forgive. but the truth is that he is always ready, even eager to forgive. He is "a God ready to pardon, gracious and merciful, slow to anger, and of great kindness." (Nehemiah 9:17.)

Too often we think of forgiveness in terms of months or years of pleading. But all that time is not required to persuade God to forgive. Elder Hugh W. Pinnock said, "The Lord forgives us in a millionth of a millisecond." When that wonderful statement was challenged by one who could not believe such a gift was possible, Elder Pinnock said, "Well, perhaps I made a mistake: the Savior forgives us *instantly*. It doesn't even take him a millionth of a millisecond." (*BYU Speeches of the Year*, Provo, Utah: Brigham Young University Press, 1979, p. 120.)

For his anger kindleth against the wicked; they repent, and in a moment it is turned away, and they are in his favor, and he giveth them life; therefore, weeping may endure for a night, but joy cometh in the morning. (Psalms 30:5, JST.)

To the Lord our God belong mercies and forgiveness, though we have rebelled against him.
(Daniel 9:9.)

The scriptures often speak of the abundant "riches of
grace" that provide forgiveness to every repentant person.
In Christ, said Paul, "we have redemption through his
blood, the forgiveness of sins, according to the riches of
his grace." (Ephesians 1:7; See also 2:7.) Many scriptures
speak of Christ's abundant goodness, mercy and grace.
(See Exodus 34:6; 2 Corinthians 4:15; 1 Peter 1:3; Alma
18:41.) Other prophets have used the word "plenteous" to
describe the Lord's eagerness to forgive the sins we have
repented of. "For thou, Lord, art good, and ready to forgive; and plenteous in mercy unto all them that call upon
thee." (Psalms 86:5; See also Psalms 86:15; 130:7.)

The Lord is merciful and gracious, slow to
anger, and plenteous in mercy . . . neither will he
keep his anger forever.
He hath not dealt with us after our sins; nor
rewarded us according to our iniquities.
For as the heaven is high above the earth, so
great is his mercy toward them that fear him.
(Psalms 103:8-11.)

Of all the questions asked of bishops in personal inter-
views, perhaps one of the most common is, "How can I tell
when I've been forgiven?" The answer is simple, but we
often miss it and make it difficult by our unbelief. The
answer is simply to trust in the redeeming blood of Christ
and believe his promises of ready, plenteous, abundant
forgiveness. Jesus Christ promised that "he who has
repented of his sins, the same is forgiven," and "he that
repents and does the commandments of the Lord shall be
forgiven." (D&C 58:42; 1:32.) Notice that these verses do
not say what Satan would like us to think they say, that if
we try to be good, we *could* be forgiven, or that we *might*
be forgiven. What they say is that when we repent, we
shall be forgiven. This is an iron-clad, unconditional
promise from the Son of God.

The difficulty is never in persuading God to forgive us. His forgiveness is automatic. When we confess, repent and obey, he forgives. If we cannot feel the Lord's forgiveness once we have repented and put our lives back in harmony with his commandments, it is not because the Lord has withheld forgiveness, but simply because it is blocked by the overwhelming presence of our own self-condemnation. The difficulty in feeling forgiven is not that God is unwilling to forgive, but rather that he is unable to convince us that he has forgiven us because of our hardened, doubting, unbelieving hearts. The Savior left his throne of glory to suffer, bleed and die for our sins. Whether we mean it to be so or not, it is a mockery of that sacrifice when we deny ourselves the forgiveness he suffered to make possible.

It is true that God has very strict standards and that he cannot look upon sin with the least degree of allowance. (See D&C 1:31.) But it is also true that he has infinite tolerance, compassion and mercy, infinite patience and forgiveness for every repentant person. The message of Christ's atonement is that he wants to wrap us in the arms of his love and forgiveness and lead us back to Heavenly Father. "Whosoever repenteth shall find mercy," for "the Lord will be merciful unto all who call on his name." (Alma 32:13; 9:17.)

We learn much about the Lord's forgiveness from the attitude of the father in the parable of the prodigal son. What we would expect from this father, what the prodigal would expect to hear upon his return would be, "So, you've come crawling back. I hope you've learned your lesson. If you're ready to be obedient for a change and measure up to the standards around here, then you're welcome back, but don't be expecting any more handouts from me. You've had your chance and you blew it."

But that didn't happen because the father in the parable doesn't represent an earthly father. He represents the forgiving attitude of the Savior and our Heavenly Father who do not grudgingly wait till we have groveled, but welcome our repentance and bestow their forgiveness freely, eagerly.

As the prodigal approached his home, even "when he was yet a great way off, his father saw him, and had compassion and ran and fell on his neck, and kissed him."

Confessing his errors, the son said unto him, "Father, I have sinned against heaven, and in thy sight, and am no more worthy to be called thy son." But the father would have no groveling. His repentant son was to be welcomed and returned to honor. "Bring forth the best robe, and put it on him; and put a ring on his hand, and shoes on his feet," the rejoicing father commanded. "And bring hither the fatted calf, and kill it; and let us eat, and be merry: For this my son was dead, and is alive again; he was lost, and is found. And they began to be merry." (Luke 15:11-24.)

Truly the Savior is a God who is "ready to pardon"—a kind, compassionate, merciful God who has promised, "As often as my people repent will I forgive them their trespasses against me." (Mosiah 26:30; See also Moroni 6:8.)

There was a time when I thought forgiveness was impossible for me. After 30 years of spiritual defeat, I felt hopeless to overcome my addictions and my guilt. In my ignorance of the Savior and his atonement, I truly believed I was beyond the reach of his love and forgiveness. But Christ's atonement is infinite. With the possible exception of deliberate, cold-blooded murder or blasphemy against the Holy Ghost, there is no mistake we can make which cannot be erased, once we repent and change our lives.

"Erase" is a good synonym for forgive, because when God forgives a sin, erasure is exactly what happens. The sin is literally erased from the record of our lives. It is blotted out, as though it never occurred. When we stand before the bar of justice with our sins erased, we will be judged for what we are at that moment, not for what we used to be during our sinning. "Repent ye therefore," admonished Peter, "that your sins may be blotted out." (Acts 3:19.) Showing that this is exactly what he does with repented sins, Jehovah, the premortal Christ declared, "I have blotted out, as a thick cloud, thy transgressions, and, as a cloud, thy sins." (Isaiah 44:22.)

Thou hast forgiven the iniquity of thy people,
thou hast covered all their sin. (Psalms 85:2.)

Joseph Smith demonstrated that it is proper to pray for this *covering*, or *blotting out*, or divine *erasing* of our sins, when he prayed, "O Jehovah, have mercy upon this people, and as all men sin forgive the transgressions of thy people, and let them be blotted out forever." (D&C 109:34; See also Psalms 51:1, 9.)

Even more wonderful than the blotting out of our sins is the Savior's assurance that his perfect forgiveness will ultimately remove the *effects* of our sins, leaving us as pure and clean and holy as though we had never made the wrong choice. "If we confess our sins, he is faithful and just to forgive us our sins, and to cleanse us from all unrighteousness." (1 John 1:9; See also Jeremiah 33:8.) So total is the Savior's cleansing of our stains that the Prophet Micah said God will not only "have compassion upon us" and "subdue our iniquities," but, "wilt cast all their sins into the depths of the sea." (Micah 7:19.) President Spencer W. Kimball taught that "when one has washed his robes in the blood of the Lamb, they are no longer soiled." (*Ensign*, November 1980, p. 30.) Validating these promises, the Savior said of former sinners, "Behold, your sins are forgiven you; you are clean before me; therefore, lift up your heads and rejoice." (D&C 110:5.)

> And again, if ye by the grace of God are perfect in Christ, and deny not his power, then are ye sanctified in Christ by the grace of God, through the shedding of the blood of Christ, which is in the covenant of the Father unto the remission of your sins, that ye become holy, without spot. (Moroni 10:33.)

For years, well-intended gospel teachers have compared sinning to the act of driving a nail in a board, and then assumed that repentance and forgiveness are like pulling the nail out. The error of this analogy is that no matter how sincere or total the repentance, we would still have a board full of holes. This analogy does not agree with the scriptures we have considered about the Savior's forgiveness "covering," "erasing," "removing," or "blotting out" our sins. The scriptures teach that the application of Christ's atonement to our personal sins makes us clean, literally a "new creature in Christ." (2 Corinthians 5:17.)

There are no ugly scars remaining in a true disciple. Once forgiven, the past is gone. There are no ugly holes left to remind us of our mistakes. Even the saddest consequences of sins sincerely repented of and forgiven by the Savior, will be removed and made clean and whole—if not in this life, then certainly in the next.

Heather O'Brian told of forsaking her sins and feeling that God was pleased with her new life. Yet she was haunted by the feeling that "he was holding my past over my head, waiting for me to fall again." She told how comforted she was to read an article by Jeffrey R. Holland, then president of BYU, in which he spoke of the analogy of the nails in the board, but clarified that "no holes remain because after repenting we have an entirely new board." She felt even more encouraged when she realized that "the only holes that do remain are the ones in Christ's hands and feet. His sacrifice was complete." (*New Era*, April, 1990, pp. 11-14.) How could the Savior say "I, even I, am he that blotteth out thy transgressions," if the ugly holes were still there? (Isaiah 43:25.) He couldn't. Apostle John recorded the Savior's promise that he will "make all things new." (Revelations 21:5.)

Alma stated that "the Son of God suffereth according to the flesh that he might take upon him the sins of his people," which means that we no longer have the sin nor the scars caused by the sin. Through the power of his infinite atonement, Christ has the power to remove them from us. Alma further stated that the reason he takes them from us is so that "he might blot out their transgressions according to the power of his deliverance." (Alma 7:13.) The power of Christ's deliverance is total, infinite and perfect. "As far as the east is from the west, so far hath he removed our transgression from us." (Psalms 103:12.)

We see an example of this in the mission of the four sons of Mosiah to the Lamanites when they were converted to the Church by the thousands. But these converts faced terrible memories. Because these previously cruel Lamanites had robbed, raped and murdered the Nephites, they had a tremendous problem believing that God's forgiveness was possible for them. However, once they understood and accepted the Savior's atonement as it applied to their sins, they were freed from their feelings of guilt. One of them testified: "I also thank my God, yea, my great God, that he hath granted unto us that we might repent of these things, and also that he hath forgiven us of those our many sins and murders which we have committed, and taken away the guilt from our hearts, through the merits of his Son." (Alma 24:10.) Each of us may experience that same joy as we come into the arms of our Savior's healing, cleansing forgiveness.

After a lengthy struggle in prayer, Enos received the same blotting or erasure of his guilt. "And there came a voice unto me, saying: Enos, thy sins are forgiven thee, and thou shalt be blessed. And I, Enos, knew that God could not lie; wherefore, my guilt was swept away." (Enos 1:5-6.) These examples were included in the Book of Mormon to teach the availability of those same loving arms of forgiveness for us today.

Alma, who described himself as one of the "vilest of sinners" (Mosiah 28:4) experienced the same joy as Enos and the converted Lamanites. He stated that for three days and nights he was so "racked with the pains of a damned soul" that the thought of coming into the presence of God filled him with "inexpressible horror" and caused him to wish for total extinction so that he might escape into nothingness. (See Alma 36:12-16.) Yet, when he gave his heart to Christ and asked for the Savior's forgiveness, the guilt was so totally removed from his heart that he testified, "I could remember my pains no more" and "my soul was filled with joy as exceeding as was my pain!" (Alma 36:19-20.) This is the gift of total forgiveness which Christ is working to share with each of us. Desiring that every person reading the Book of Mormon understands that this total, perfect, healing forgiveness is real, Alma concluded: "Yea, I say unto you . . . that there could be nothing so exquisite and so bitter as were my pains. Yea, and again I say unto you . . . that on the other hand, there can be nothing so exquisite and sweet as was my joy." (Alma 36:21.)

If we still feel guilty and ashamed after proper repentance, it is because we are clinging to our past and refusing to allow the perfect, infinite, healing atonement to cleanse and erase that past and bring us into the forgiving arms of the Savior who made it all possible. Because of the Savior's sacrifice for us "mercy can satisfy the demands of justice, and encircles them in the arms of safety" and forgiveness. (Alma 34:16.)

> Wo be unto the Gentiles, saith the Lord God of Hosts! For notwithstanding I shall lengthen out mine arm unto them from day to day, they will deny me; nevertheless, I will be merciful unto them, saith the Lord God, if they will repent and come unto me; for mine arm is lengthened out all the day long, saith the Lord God of Hosts. (2 Nephi 28:32.)

One of the kindest revelations is the Savior's explanation of what he does after forgiving and erasing our sins. He actually dismisses them from his memory! This fact is, perhaps, the greatest miracle of divine forgiveness, yet it is also the hardest to believe. "Behold," said the Savior, "he who has repented of his sins, the same is forgiven, and I, the Lord, remember them no more." (D&C 58:42.) He also said, "I will be merciful to their unrighteousness, and their sins and their iniquities will I remember no more." (Hebrews 8:12; See also 10:17.) To Jeremiah he said, "I will forgive their iniquity, and I will remember their sin no more." (Jeremiah 31:34.)

I once heard an interview on the radio in which a man mentioned that he had four sons, two of whom were adopted. He claimed that he could never remember which two. When I heard that, I thought to myself, "That's ridiculous. No one could be so pure in their love as to forget which children were adopted. No way!" Immediately, the Spirit came into my mind and whispered: "No, Steve, you are wrong. Not only is this possible, it is also an example of what God has said and you have doubted—that when God forgives, he also forgets and remembers the sin no more. You have questioned how a God who knows everything could really forget your sins."

That was true. I had puzzled over that.

And then there came into my mind the impression of a scene. It seemed as if I were standing by the gates of the celestial city as throngs of people entered it. They were beautiful, dressed in radiant white, with indescribable joy radiating from their faces. Then I realized that Heavenly Father and Mother were also there with Jesus, watching them enter. I didn't see them, but I could sense their presence and hear what they said. It seemed as if I heard the Savior say to Mother and Father, "Isn't it marvelous to think that some of these people were once so rebellious and filthy that we actually had to excommunicate them from our Church? And now, here they are in beauty and perfection, and they will be with us forever and ever."

And then our Heavenly Mother turned to him and asked, "Jesus, which ones?"

I heard the Savior reply, "I don't remember." (Steven A. Cramer, *Conquering Your Own Goliaths*, Salt Lake City, Deseret Book, 1988, pp. 78-79.)

How can a God who knows everything really forget our past? He doesn't. The Lord never said he would *forget* our forgiven sins. What he said is that, through a conscious, deliberate choice, he puts them out of his mind by choosing to no longer *remember* or give importance to them. What is important to the Lord once we have repented is not what we did, but what we learned from the mistakes and how we are going to live from now on. No matter how filthy or wicked our past has been, we have this confidence, that our future is just as spotless as the Prophet's.

So total is the dismissal of our past from Christ's memory that when we come before him in judgment, forgiven sins "that he hath committed, they shall not be mentioned unto him." (Ezekiel 18:22.) God does not keep score! (Psalms 79:8; 130:3-4.) Why doesn't he keep score? I believe it is because he doesn't want his mind cluttered with the irrelevancies of the past. "I, even I, am he that blotteth out thy transgressions for mine own sake, and will not remember thy sins." (Isaiah 43:25.) For similar references about the Lord dismissing such things "for his own sake," see: Psalms 23:3; 25:11; 31:3; Isaiah 48:9; Ephesians 4:32; D&C 64:3.

If a divine, perfect being chooses to dismiss our repented, forgiven sins from his memory "for his own sake," what right do we have to pollute our minds by keeping track of what Christ has removed? Elder Marvin J. Ashton said, "The Lord promised that he will forgive and remember no more when the process of repentance is complete. If the Lord will do that for us, why should we not so do for ourselves?" ("Roadblocks to Progress," *Ensign*, May 1979, p. 68.) And Theodore M. Burton said, "That forgiveness which comes from our Heavenly Father is so complete that he will not even call to mind the sins we have committed. His forgiveness is so all-inclusive that the Lord will not even remember those sins. (*Ensign*, May 1983, p. 71.)

Many sincere Christians misunderstand this gift of the Savior's forgiveness. They feel ashamed simply because they need his gift. Needing the Savior shouldn't make us feel inferior. It only shows that we are mortal and that we are learning a better way. Our Savior and Heavenly Father rejoice when we come to them with our burdens.

Scripture says, "Blessed is he whose transgression is forgiven, whose sin is covered." (Romans 4:7; See also Psalms 32:1.) Nowhere do the scriptures say, or even hint, "Blessed is he who never needs forgiveness," because there is no such person.

Scripture also says, "Blessed are they who will repent and turn unto me . . . ." (Helaman 13:11.) And, "Blessed are they who will repent and hearken unto the voice of the Lord their God; for these are they that shall be saved." (Helaman 12:23.) Nowhere do the scriptures say or even hint, "Blessed is he who never needs to repent," for only Christ was in that position.

Who will win the celestial kingdom and the privilege of dwelling with God for eternity? Will it be those who never needed repentance or forgiveness? No! That is Satan's falsification. This lie is designed to discourage us from repenting and seeking forgiveness because he knows "how great is [the Lord's] joy in the soul that repenteth." (D&C 18:13.) The Savior taught that the purpose of the gospel and the church is for "the convincing of many of their sins, that they may come unto repentance, and that they may come unto the kingdom of my Father." (D&C 18:44.) So, who goes to heaven? Repentant sinners! When that joyful day arrives we will each be met by the welcoming arms of our Savior and Heavenly Father.

> What man of you, having an hundred sheep, if he lose one of them, doth not leave the ninety and nine in the wilderness, and go after that which is lost, until he find it?
>
> And when he hath found it, he layeth it on his shoulders, rejoicing.
>
> And when he cometh home, he calleth together his friends and neighbors, saying unto them, Rejoice with me; for I have found my sheep which was lost. (Luke 15:4-6.)

Part Two

Growing Closer to The Savior

Admitting Our Need for Christ

The purpose of this book is to lead the reader into the arms of Christ's love. Some people have expressed the opinion that it is wrong to seek a personal relationship with Christ. They feel that we should keep our distance, that we should not expect him to be involved in our day-to-day lives. Perhaps they feel that God and Christ are so far above us in holiness that they would be offended by our desire for a personal relationship with them. However, the scriptures and the prophets teach that it is not only *possible* to be close to the Savior, but that he actually *invites* and welcomes our friendship and that this personal relationship is an essential part of true discipleship.

"God is faithful, by whom ye were called unto the fellowship of his Son, Jesus Christ our Lord." (1 Corinthians 1:9.) The scriptures use the word "fellowship" carefully and intentionally. Fellowship is defined as friendliness, comradeship, as personal companionship and association. (*Webster's Seventh New Collegiate Dictionary*, Springfield, Mass.: G. & C. Merriam Co., 1963.) This fellowship, or personal relationship is to be sought with both the Father and the Savior, for "truly our fellowship is with the Father, and with his Son Jesus Christ." (1 John 1:3.)

When one is a disciple of Jesus Christ, there comes a relationship to him that brings nearness. (*Ensign*, June 1980, p. 44.)

115

What we need to remember is that, in essence, Christianity is a relationship, not (just) a set of rules or a list of behaviors. (Stanley C. Baldwin, *Bruised But Not Broken*, Portland, Oregon: Multnomah Press, 1985, p. 41.)

"Do we fully realize that Jesus is to be the center of our lives?" asked Hugh W. Pinnock. "Only the Savior can be our Savior, and that relationship is always personal. We go to him alone. He accepts us that way only. There is no other way." (*Ensign*, May 1989, p. 12.) Brigham Young made a statement that helps us understand the intimacy of the personal relationship we should be seeking. He said, "The greatest and most important of all requirements of our Father in Heaven and of his Son Jesus Christ . . . is to believe in Jesus Christ, confess him, seek to know him, cling to him, make friends with him. Take a course to open and keep open a communication with your elder brother or file leader—our Savior." (*Journal of Discourses*, Vol. 8, p. 339, as quoted in the Relief Society Manual, 1982, p. 24.)

Adding to Brigham's admonition, President Ezra Taft Benson said we should "Establish a deep and abiding relationship with the Lord Jesus Christ." (*Ensign*, November 1988, p. 97.) And as he concluded his 1988 Christmas message, President Benson said, "May the Babe of Bethlehem be the object of our worship and the focus of our lives during this blessed Christmas season— and always." (*Ensign*, February, 1989, p. 74.) President Benson also said:

We have an increasing number who have been convinced, through the Book of Mormon, that Jesus is the Christ. Now we need an increasing number who will use the Book of Mormon to become committed to Christ. Let us continually reread the Book of Mormon so that we might more fully come to Christ, be committed to him, centered in him, and consumed in him. We must be close to Christ, we must daily take his name upon us, always remember him, and keep his command- ments." (*New Era*, April 1988, pp. 6-7.)

Being close to Christ, "clinging" to him and being "consumed" in him are powerful phrases indeed. So is the word "cleave." Cleave is used many times in the scriptures to describe the personal relationship we should seek with the Savior, who said, "Cleave unto me with all your heart." (D&C 11:19.) Prophets through the ages have encouraged, even commanded us to do exactly that as we seek to know and love the Savior. "Ye shall . . . love the Lord your God, to walk in all his ways, and to cleave unto him," Moses commanded. (Deuteronomy 11:22.) Jacob encouraged us to "come with full purpose of heart, and cleave unto God as he cleaveth unto you." (Jacob 6:5.)

Ultimately then, nothing in our life is going to be right until we are right with the Savior. As Apostle Howard W. Hunter said, "Please remember this one thing. If our lives and our faith are centered upon Jesus Christ and his restored gospel, nothing can ever go permanently wrong. On the other hand, if our lives are not centered on the Savior and his teachings, no other success can ever be permanently right." (*Devotional Speeches of The Year*, Provo, Utah: B.Y.U. Press, 1988-89, p. 112.)

So the question facing us as we come to part two of this book, the choice we each must make is whether to drift through mortality satisfied to merely "be active" in church and do the outward things required of us, or whether to reach higher, and enjoy the marvelous privilege of developing a personal relationship with the Savior that will lead us to a closer relationship with Heavenly Father.

Jesus declared that the essence of eternal life is to truly, intimately know him and our Heavenly Father. "And this is life eternal, that they might know thee the only true God, and Jesus Christ, whom thou hast sent." (John 17:3.) Elder Bernard P. Brockbank said, "No other success can compensate for failing to know the living God and the living Jesus Christ." (*Ensign*, July 1972, p. 123.) This is speaking of far more than merely knowing *about* them. It means that we must come to know them personally, as our very best friends.

It is one thing to know *about* God and another to know *him*. We know them, in the sense of gaining eternal life, when we enjoy and experience the same things they do. To know God is to think what he thinks, to feel what he feels, to have the power he possesses, to comprehend the truths he understands, and to do what he does. Those who know God become like him, and have his kind of life, which is eternal life. (Bruce R. McConkie, *Doctrinal New Testament Commentary*, 3 Vols., Salt Lake City: Bookcraft, Inc., 1971, 1:762; emphasis added.)

The path to *knowing* Christ is to *receive* him into our hearts, into our deepest emotions and day-to-day life. "Strait is the gate, and narrow the way that leadeth unto the exaltation and continuation of the lives," Christ warned, "and few there be that find it, because ye receive me not in the world neither do ye know me." (D&C 132:22.) One prophet lamented, "The Lord hath a controversy with the inhabitants of the land, because there is no . . . knowledge of God in the land." (Hosea 4:1.) Another prophet quoted the Lord: "Let him that glorieth glory in this, that he understandeth and knoweth me, that I am the Lord which exercise lovingkindness, judgment, and righteousness, in the earth: for in these things I delight, saith the Lord." (Jeremiah 9:24.)

"As with mortal relationships, we need to develop a close and personal relationship with the Lord to know him." (Relief Society Manual, 1982, p. 25.) Referring to the importance of learning to know Christ through our personal relationship, President Marion G. Romney said, "Such knowledge is essential to exaltation. It is more than a mental concept. It comes only through personal two-way communication with the Lord." (*Learning For The Eternities*, Comp. George J. Romney, Salt Lake City, Utah: Deseret Book, 1977, p. 9.)

How well do we actually know our Savior? How often do we think of him during our weekly activities? He has promised to make himself known personally to every person who comes to him in humility and submissive obedience. "If ye receive me in the world, then shall ye know me, and shall receive your exaltation; that where I am ye shall be also." (D&C 132:23.) Speaking of the day we each come before him in judgment, the Savior said, "In my name are they called; and if they know me they shall come forth, and shall have a place eternally at my right hand," but "if they know not the name by which they are called, they cannot have place in the kingdom of my Father." (Mosiah 26:24; D&C 18:25.)

Let us not be so foolish as to believe we can attain exaltation or learn to know the Savior merely by attending meetings. He is talking about a relationship far more personal than that. "We can come to know the Savior better than we know any other person on earth. The Savior can have, and indeed must have, a greater impact on our lives than the combined impact of everyone else we know!" (George W. Pace, *What It Means To Know Christ*, Provo, Utah: Council Press, 1981, p. 2.)

While the path to exaltation is strait and narrow, "Broad is the gate, and wide the way that leadeth to the deaths; and many there are that go in thereat, because they receive me not, neither do they abide in my law." (D&C 132:25.) In the parable of the ten virgins, the five latecomers petitioned, "Lord, Lord, open unto us." (Matthew 25:11.) Regretfully they were denied entrance into the presence of the Lord. The reason given was: "Verily I say unto you, Ye know me not." (Matthew 25:12 JST.)

In seeking to know God we are only relearning what we once knew. "I want to tell you, each and every one of you," said Brigham Young, "that you are well acquainted with God our Heavenly Father, or the great Elohim. You are well acquainted with him, for there is not a soul of you but what has lived in his house and dwelt with him year after year; and yet you are seeking to become acquainted with him, when the fact is, you have merely forgotten what you did know." (*Discourses of Brigham Young*, Salt Lake City, Utah: Deseret Book, 1951, p. 50.) Realizing this should encourage us in our quest.

When we see our Father in Heaven (again) we shall know Him; and the recollection that we were once with Him and that He was our Father will come back to us, and we will fall upon His neck, and He will fall upon us, and we will kiss each other. (*Gospel Truth; Discourses and Writings of President George Q. Cannon*, sel. Jerrald L. Newquist, Vol. 1, Salt Lake City: Zion's Book Store, 1957, p. 3.)

In seeking to reclaim that personal acquaintance now hidden by the veil, we cannot go directly to the Father, but only through Jesus Christ. The Savior has given a strict commandment that we do not attempt to approach Heavenly Father without going through him. "I am the way" back to the Father, he declared, and "no man cometh unto the Father, but by me." Indeed, "I give unto you this commandment—that no man shall come unto the Father but by me or by my word, which is my law, saith the Lord." (John 14:6; D&C 132:12.) Elder Bernard P. Brockbank said, "The answers to knowing God the Eternal Father are found in and through Jesus Christ. In order to know God the Eternal Father, we must receive that knowledge . . . through Jesus Christ, who is the mediator between God and man." (*Ensign*, July 1972, p. 121.) This principle was echoed by Elder Bruce R. McConkie when he said, "We know the Father by coming to an understanding of the Son." (*Ensign*, April 1975, p. 71.)

Elder Neal A. Maxwell said that "when we have the spirit with us, it means we have achieved significant Christ-centerdness in our lives, for we cannot be close to one member of the Godhead without being close to all three." (*Notwithstanding My Weakness*, Salt Lake City, Utah: Deseret Book, 1981, p. 112.) Surely this is what the Savior had in mind when he stated, "He that receiveth me receiveth him that sent me," and "he that receiveth me receiveth my Father." (John 13:20; D&C 84:37.)

The Savior has used many compelling examples to illustrate the depth of dependence he wants us to enjoy in our relationship with him. Consider, for example, the relationship of dependence that exists between a tool and its craftsman:

Shall the axe boast itself against him that heweth therewith? Or shall the saw magnify itself against him that shaketh it? (Isaiah 10:15.)

Shall the work say of him that made it, He made me not? Or shall the thing framed say of him that framed it, He had no understanding? (Isaiah 29:16.)

Isaiah used the example of tools because it is obvious that no matter how perfect the tool is, it can never, by itself, accomplish any good. To accomplish its purpose, the tool must be placed in the hands of a skilled crafts- man. Isaiah was not concerned about tools however, but about our relationship with God. Catherine Thomas said, "We may defy our nothingness and attempt to become something without God. Yet, when we can finally admit that we are nothing without God, the Savior invites us to lay on the altar the great burden of trying to do everything on our own." (*Ensign*, June 1987, p. 6.) We must be will- ing to set aside our pride and acknowledge that with God holding us in his hand and guiding us in life's experience, we will always be superior to that which we could achieve without him. Going through life insisting on becoming "a self-made man," is foolish. Can we not be wise enough to surrender our making to the Master Craftsman? "Know ye that the Lord he is God: it is he that hath made us, and not we ourselves." (Psalms 100:3.)

Hugh W. Pinnock said further: "We function best in an environment of freedom. We are free when we are indepen- dent, and we are totally independent only when we are completely dependent upon the Savior." (*Devotional Speeches of the Year*, Provo, Utah: Brigham Young University Press, 1979, p. 116.)

As we strive for success in living the gospel it is natu- ral to center our thoughts and emotions, our confidence and reliance upon ourselves. After all, it is our duty to do right and it is our duty to do well. We should realize, how- ever, that this self-centered philosophy was one of the main points of the anti-Christ doctrine preached by Korihor and others like him. Korihor taught that reliance upon Jesus Christ "is the effect of a frenzied mind; and this derangement of your minds," he said, "comes because of the traditions of your fathers, which lead you away into a belief of things which are not so." (Alma 30:16.) As Korihor went about teaching people to rely solely upon themselves rather than upon Christ, he taught the popular and appealing humanistic doctrine that "every man fared in this life according to the management of the creature; therefore every man prospered according to his genius, and that every man conquered according to his strength." (Alma 30:17.)

In contrast to this anti-Christ philosophy of depending upon ourselves instead of Christ, President Spencer W. Kimball stated "the man who leans heavily on his Lord becomes the master of self and can accomplish anything he sets out to do." (*The Miracle of Forgiveness*, Salt Lake City, Utah: Bookcraft Inc., 1969, p. 176.) The Book of Mormon speaks of a people who followed Korihor's self-reliance philosophy. "And because of . . . their boastings in their own strength, they were left in their own strength; therefore they did not prosper, but were afflicted and smitten." (Helaman 4:13.)

> One of the most important realizations any person can have is coming face to face with his or her mortality, becoming painfully aware of his or her weakness and infirmities. It is only as we sense our inadequacies, as we admit our own human limitations, that we eagerly turn to him who offers deliverance and relief from the weighty burden of sin.
>
> Only those who come to realize their spiritual bankruptcy—who recognize the wide chasm between their own labors and the perfections of Deity, and who resolve to draw upon the infinite powers of him who is mighty to save—only these grow in those spiritual graces which lead to life eternal.
>
> Man cannot justify himself. He cannot sanctify himself. And he certainly cannot perfect himself. The transformations from a fallen nature to a spiritual nature, from worldliness to perfection are accomplished because divine powers bring them to pass. They are acts of grace. (Robert L. Millet, *By Grace Are We Saved*, Salt Lake City, Utah: Bookcraft, 1989, p. 86.)

Of course it is necessary that we use our own strengths and abilities to do as much for ourselves as we can. But it is also imperative that we recognize that no one can ever do enough, by his own efforts alone, to live the obedient life that will result in exaltation. If we could, why would we need the Savior? Consider the following words from the 1969-70 Gospel Doctrine Manual: "Only in him can any man find the strength, the power and ability to live a godly life. Only in Christ is there power to transform the human mind and the human heart. Only in Jesus Christ can any man learn the truth of what he is and how he can be changed from what he is to do the good for which he hopes. (*In His Footsteps Today*, Salt Lake City, Utah: Deseret Sunday School Union, 1969, p. 4.)

> Only Jesus Christ is qualified to provide that hope, that confidence, and that strength to overcome the world and rise above our human failings.
> Faith in him is more than mere acknowledgment that he lives. It is more than professing belief. *Faith in Jesus Christ consists of complete reliance on Him.* (Ezra Taft Benson, *Ensign*, November 1983, p. 6; 8; emphasis added.)

Isaiah also used the example of the potter's clay to illustrate our dependence upon Christ. "But now, O Lord, thou art our Father; we are the clay, and thou our potter; and we are all the work of thy hand. Shall the clay say to him that fashioneth it, What makest thou?" (Isaiah 64:8; 45:9; see also Romans 9:20-21.) God compared to a potter? Man compared to a lump of clay? What a strange analogy this would be if we did not understand that Isaiah was only teaching us how much we need the Savior in our daily life. "Behold, as the clay is in the potter's hand, so are ye in mine hand, O house of Israel." (Jeremiah 18:6.)

When we judge ourselves in terms of a finished vessel, we feel inferior and unworthy because we know that we are far from perfection. But when we see ourselves as unfinished clay in the hands of the Master Potter, we have the confident assurance that he will make of us a far more beautiful vessel than we could ever imagine or make of ourselves. And because we know that he will never stop working with us until he has molded us to our perfect capacity, we can exercise the patience to love and accept ourselves as he continues to fashion us.

The scriptures also compare the dependence we should feel toward Christ with a child's dependence upon its parents and the totally dependent, trusting relationship between a sheep and its shepherd. But the most compelling of all analogies is that drawn by the Savior when he stated that our relationship with him should be as essential as that of a branch to a vine.

> I am the true vine, and my Father is the husbandman.
>
> I am the vine, ye are the branches: He that abideth in me, and I in him, the same bringeth forth much fruit: *for without me ye can do nothing.*
>
> Abide in me, and I in you. As the branch cannot bear fruit of itself, except it abide in the vine; no more can ye, except ye abide in me. (John 15:1, 5, 4; emphasis added.)

What does it mean to be so close to Jesus Christ that we are "abiding" in him as literally as the nourishing sap that flows from the vine into the branches? It means, as Elder James E. Faust counselled, that "we should earnestly seek not just to know about the Master, but to strive, as He invited, to be one with him." (*Ensign*, November 1976, p. 58.)

> Our goal for our relationship with Jesus Christ may be summed up on the Lord's counsel to Enoch, "Walk with me." (*Ensign*, June 1980, p. 44; see also Moses 6:34.)

The scriptures warn of the danger of neglecting this personal relationship. Continuing his analogy of the dependence of the branches upon the vine, the Savior warned, "If a man abide not in me, he is cast forth as a branch, and is withered; and men gather them, and cast them into the fire, and they are burned." (John 15:6.) Mormon warned, "Except they should cleave unto the

Lord their God, they must unavoidably perish." (Helaman 4:25.) David said, "They that are far from thee shall perish . . . but it is good for me to draw near to God." (Psalms 73:27-28.) And Vaughn J. Featherstone, of the First Quorum of Seventy said, "Number one on our agenda, above all else, is faith in Christ. Whenever we find problems in the Church, we usually find them under one of two umbrellas or canopies, either transgression or lack of faith in Christ." (*Devotional Speeches of the Year*, Provo, Utah: Brigham Young University Press, 1982-83, p. 145.)

Perhaps the depth of fellowship which is offered by Christ is best described by the frequency with which he refers to us as his friends. Abraham was often called "the friend of God," and that is the relationship which Jesus wants to establish with each of us. "Henceforth I call you not servants . . . but I have called you friends." (John 15:15.) "And again I say unto you, my friends, for from henceforth I shall call you friends, it is expedient that I give unto you this commandment, that ye become even as my friends in days when I was with them, traveling to preach the gospel in my power." (D&C 84:77.) Malcom S. Jeppsen, of the Quorum of Seventy said:

> Cultivate our Savior and Redeemer Jesus Christ as your friend above all. Being his friend will without exception lift your vision and bring you comfort, guidance, peace. Just think! With Jesus as your friend, you may receive increased strength and testimony that will uphold you against temptations when they arise. Above all, be a friend of the Savior. If you have not done so previously, now is the time to let him know you consider him your true friend and that you will be a true friend of his. (*Ensign*, May 1990, p. 45.)

In the Doctrine and Covenants the Savior refers to us as his friends over a dozen times. Why not "my servants"? Or "my disciples"? Or "my followers"? There is a great difference between these titles and the warm, inviting title of "friend." President Spencer W. Kimball said, "On those days when earthly friends may disappoint you, remember

that the Savior of mankind has described Himself as your
friend. He is your very best friend." (*New Era*, July 1980,
p. 10.) But can I qualify for such a high invitation? Can it
really apply to me? Certainly. Christ himself set the simple
standard when he said, "Ye are my friends, if ye do whatsoever I command you." (John 15:14.)

Elder Charles Didier, of the First Quorum of Seventy
said, "One of the real purposes of life is to become a friend
of the Mediator, our Savior and Redeemer, and not only
understand his mission but also support it and then qualify to be called his friend, his disciple, and to enter into
the presence of his Father. Are we strong enough to accept
friendship with Christ? Be committed to be his friend? The
covenant we made through baptism is a contract to
become a friend of God. If you have not done so previously, now is the time to become friends of God." (*Ensign*,
November 1983, pp. 23-24.)

Marion D. Hanks has lamented that "For some of us, a
reason for unhappiness is that 'the world is too much with
us.' The struggle for what we need or for more than we
need exhausts our time and energy. We pursue pleasure
or entertainment, or become over involved in associations
of civic matters. Of course, people need recreation, need to
be achieving, need to contribute; but if these come at the
cost of friendship with Christ, the price is much too high."
(*Conference Report*, April 1972, p. 127.)

Now we must come to the question of how to develop
the relationship with Christ that will lead us back to our
Heavenly Father's fellowship.

I am sorry I cannot tell you how; it is an individual
quest. I can only share my personal quest and suggest
essential ingredients in the process.

When I first recognized the spiritual bankruptcy in my
own life, I discovered that all my problems were rooted in
my lack of relationship with Jesus Christ. I felt as helpless
as a baby at the foot of Mount Everest because after a life-
time in the Church, after having read the scriptures many
times, I discovered, to my shame, that I knew very little
about the Savior. I had been "active" all my life, but that
activity had failed to develop a love and appreciation for
him. Without realizing it, I had taken him for granted all

my life. I knew almost nothing of his atonement. I certainly did not understand its application to my personal sins and burdens. To my astonishment, I realized I did not know my Savior as a person. I knew nothing of the arms of his love. Jesus Christ was literally a stranger to me!

But the most devastating realization was that I did not know how to find him.

Coming from an engineering background, I wanted a checklist of things to do so that when the list was completed, presto, I would have won him as my friend. I went to a trusted friend, a man who was closer to Jesus than any person I knew. I took with me a notebook with over a hundred questions about the process I must follow, all the things I must do and how long it would take. In less than five minutes with my friend, I closed my list of questions. This man who is a true friend of Christ taught me that I didn't need all those answers. All I needed to do was trust the one who is *the* answer: my Savior. It is not for the sheep to command or direct the Shepherd. It is not for the tool or the clay to direct the craftsman. It was not for me to engineer the transformation of my own soul. The Savior is the one who is in charge. It is *his* job to do the saving, the refining, the tutoring. It is *his* job to do the leading, *ours* to do the following.

What a joy it was to learn to "let go and let God." I found him willing and anxious to guide me. I learned trust as I took those first tentative steps, jubilant to discover that he never abandoned me, never left me to wander in darkness or confusion. As long as I placed him first in my priorities, he was there to guide each step.

The nine chapters that follow contain essential steps that we all must follow, essential ingredients in the process. I know by my own experience that they are each a part of the formula, but they do not present the whole formula. That is not my privilege nor right. The path of application, the sequence of refining experiences through which each of us must travel is individual and requires personal revelation. The Holy Ghost provides that personal revelation to each of us. The New Testament disciples were terrified of having Christ leave them because they mistakenly thought it meant they would be on their own, left alone. To calm those fears he gently taught them the role of the Holy Ghost.

> The Comforter, which is the Holy Ghost, whom the Father will send in my name, he shall teach you all things," and "he will guide you into all truth: for he shall not speak of himself; but whatsoever he shall hear, that shall he speak. (John 14:26; 16:13.)

Would you draw close to your Heavenly Father and Savior? Would you seek to become a personal friend of Jesus Christ? Then do whatever it takes to make the Holy Ghost your constant companion and he will guide you through whatever experiences and refinements are necessary. You do not need to *know* as much as to *trust.* Jesus Christ is waiting to welcome you into the arms of his love and fellowship. As your personal Shepherd, he knows the exact path you must walk, and if you are willing to place yourself in his keeping, he will guide you each step of the way. Remember, He is THE WAY!

> But if from thence thou shalt seek the Lord thy God, thou shalt find him, if thou seek him with all thy heart and with all thy soul. (Deuteronomy 4:29.)

Growing Closer
By Claiming
The Promises

In part one of this book we considered hundreds of scriptural portraits of our Savior's and Heavenly Father's love. Each declaration of their divine attributes is, in effect, a promise of the way we can expect them to relate to us. Simply knowing *about* the promises, however, will not change our lives. If we want to draw closer to our Savior, we must not only learn to trust his promises as true and dependable, but also how to apply them to our personal situations.

Our Heavenly Father and Savior desire to treat everyone equally, without partiality, "for there is no respect of persons with God," and "He inviteth them all to come unto him and partake of his goodness; and he denieth none that come unto him . . . and all are alike unto God." (Romans 2:11; 2 Nephi 26:33.) As a child of God, you have the right to claim any principle or promise you find in the scriptures. They apply to *you* just as much as if God had spoken them to you personally, because, in reality, he did. When the Lord places the record of his dealings with specific individuals or groups of people in the scriptures, he does so to show that we have the right and privilege to lay claim on every promise or principle we find there, for "What I say unto one I say unto all." (D&C 61:36; also 82:5.)

It is so vital to our spiritual progress that we believe this universal application of his promises that Christ has made it a commandment to interpret them this way. "I give

unto you a commandment," he said, "that what I say unto
one I say unto all." (D&C 61:18; emphasis added.) Having
been commanded to consider all his promises applicable to
our own situations, we have no excuse to dismiss or ratio-
nalize them away. "To unlock Old Testament prophecy," for
example, "readers first need to relate to the scriptures and
assume that God is speaking forth personally to them,"
said Victor L. Ludlow, director of Bible studies and associ-
ate professor of ancient scripture at Brigham Young
University (*Ensign*, October 1990, p. 60.)

> For whatsoever things were written aforetime
> were written for *our* learning, that *we* through
> patience and comfort of the scriptures might (also)
> have hope. (Romans 15:4; emphasis added.)

Brother Ludlow continued, "If readers think the
prophecies, warnings, and promises apply only to others,
the scriptures remain distant, foreign, and hidden, and
their great power is never unlocked. Since all of us in the
Church are inheritors of the promises made to the house
of Israel . . . we can read them as if Isaiah, Moses, and
other prophets were not only speaking about us, but to
us." (*Ensign*, October 1990, p. 60.)

Dr. Dean Byrd, field manager for the LDS Social
Services has likewise suggested that we can better feel the
Savior's love for us, even in our weakness, "by reading the
scriptures in a personalized way. For example," he said, "we
could read John 3:16-17, 'For God so loved [me], that he
gave his only begotten Son, that [believing in him, I] should
not perish, but have everlasting life. For God sent not his
Son into the world to condemn [me]; but that [I] through
him might be saved." (*Ensign*, September 1990, p. 53.)

But there is an even better way to personalize the
scriptures and that is by actually inserting our own name
into the verse. As Robert J. Matthews, Dean of religious
education at Brigham Young University said, "There are
hundreds of promises from the Lord that are so casually
stated that unless one is alerted to them, they almost go
unnoticed. It is in these quiet promises that we can substitute our own name for those given in the revelation. Put

your name in front of it and the promise is yours." (*Church News*, September 2, 1989, p. 5.)

The scripture that inspired this book is D&C 6:20 which says, "Be faithful and diligent in keeping the commandments of God and I will encircle thee in the arms of my love." I loved this promise and hoped it was true, but I never experienced it until I put my name into it and claimed it as mine. Look what a difference it makes to add your name:

> Steven [insert your name] Be faithful and diligent in keeping the commandments of God and [Steven,] I will encircle you in the arms of my love.

Not only is it important to "personalize" the promises with our own name, but it is equally important to build our faith to the point that we believe with absolute certainty that God is going to fulfill those promises exactly as he said, for "his purposes fail not, neither are there any who can stay his hand," because "he hath all power unto the fulfilling of all his words." (D&C 76:3; 1 Nephi 9:6.) God certainly has infinite power with which to fulfill his promises, but there is even greater reason to place our total trust in him, and that is his divine guarantee to do exactly as he has promised.

> For I will fulfill my promises which I have made unto the children of men. (2 Nephi 10:17.)

> And as the words have gone forth out of my mouth even so shall they be fulfilled. (D&C 29:30.)

> Steven (insert your name) "What I the Lord have spoken, I have spoken, and [Steven,] I excuse not myself; and though the heavens and the earth pass away, my word shall not pass away, but shall all be fulfilled." (D&C 1:38.)

The Savior has repeated this message often because he knows how easy it is to doubt and because he wants us to trust him and rely upon his promises. "He fulfilleth the words which he hath given, and he lieth not, but fulfilleth all his words." (3 Nephi 27:18.) "I have spoken it," the Lord declared, and "I will also bring it to pass; I have purposed it, I will also do it." (Isaiah 46:11.) He gave his promises to encourage us to come to him and draw upon his power and love and he is prepared to deliver exactly as he has promised, "For as I, the Lord God, liveth, even so my words cannot return void, for as they go forth out of my mouth they must be fulfilled." (Moses 4:30.)

"Now the decrees of God are unalterable," and "it is impossible for him to deny his word." (Alma 41:8; Alma 11:34.) Elder Glen L. Rudd said, "Faith is simply knowing that the Lord is there and that He will keep His promises to those who humbly approach Him." (*Ensign*, January 1989, p. 71.) "I, the Lord, promise the faithful and cannot lie." (D&C 62:6.) President N. Eldon Tanner said, "All I can do is take him at his word . . . he did not say anything he did not mean. He made no promise that he is not prepared to keep." (*Outstanding Stories by General Authorities*, comp. Leon R. Hartshorn, Salt Lake City, Utah: Deseret Book, 1970, p. 209.)

God's promises never fail. Every time we obey his law, every time we make claim upon a promise we find in his word, every time we allow his word to be fulfilled in our lives, we add another defeat to Satan and his hosts who chose to believe that God's word and plan would not work, and who try constantly to dissuade our belief as well.

> So shall my word be that goeth forth out of my mouth: it shall not return unto me void, but it shall accomplish that which I please, and it shall prosper in the thing whereto I sent it. (Isaiah 55:11.)

The Savior has sent his word to change our lives and if we will accept the promises, if we will claim them as ours, his words shall not return to him void, but will be fruitful in blessing us with the transformations he intended to accomplish. If you have difficulty believing a promise you find in the scriptures, if the overwhelming circumstances of your present defeat make the promise seem impossible, try placing your faith in the Savior who made the promise.

Jesus Christ has put his honor and integrity on the line when he said, "I cannot deny my word," and "Who am I, saith the Lord, that have promised and have not fulfilled?" (D&C 39:16; 58:31.)

Not only can we place unqualified trust in every promise we read in God's word, but we may also expect to have them "confirmed" by having them fulfilled in our own experience, for "whosoever shall believe in my name, doubting nothing, unto him will I confirm all my words, even unto the ends of the earth." (Mormon 9:25.)

> And behold, I, the Lord, declare unto you, and my words are sure and shall not fail, that they shall obtain it . . . [for] . . . all things must come to pass in their time. (D&C 64:31-32.)

> And thus we see how merciful and just are all the dealings of the Lord, to the fulfilling of all his words unto the children of men. (Alma 50:19.)

Growing Closer Through the Memory Covenant

One of the most essential keys to knowing the Savior and drawing closer to him is simply to train ourselves to think about him more often. President David O. McKay taught, "What you sincerely in your heart think of Christ will determine what you are, will largely determine what your acts will be." (*Gospel Ideals*, 7th Abridged Edition, Salt Lake City, Utah: *Improvement Era*, 1953, p. 234.) Our relationship with Christ depends not only upon *what* we think of Christ, but also upon *how often* we think of him. The more we meditate and ponder and remember Christ, the closer we will feel to him. Thinking about him often closes the door to other preoccupations and opens the door to our hearts, welcoming him to enter.

It is so important to keep the Lord focused in our daily remembrance that this command is one of the major themes in scripture, occurring almost six hundred times. For example: Steven (insert your name) "Remember the greatness of the Holy One of Israel." (2 Nephi 9:40.) "Remember his marvelous works that he hath done." (Psalms 105:5.) "I would that ye should remember and always retain in remembrance, the greatness of God . . . and his goodness and long-suffering towards you." (Mosiah 4:11.) "Beware that thou forget not the Lord thy God." (Deuteronomy 8:11.)

Nephi stated that the reason he kept such meticulous records of the Lord's dealings with his people was so that

"I might persuade them that they would remember the Lord their Redeemer." (1 Nephi 19:18.) And Peter believed this was so important that he felt his mission was: "As long as I am in this tabernacle, to stir you up by putting you in remembrance." (2 Peter 1:13.)

The Savior is so concerned that we keep him focused in our daily thoughts that he actually keeps a written record of those who do so. "And a book of remembrance was written before him for them that feared the Lord, and that thought upon his name." (3 Nephi 24:16; see also Malachi 3:16.) We are told that when Christ returns again, those whose names are in this record will be singled out for special greeting. "Yea, when thou comest down, and the mountains flow down at thy presence, thou shalt meet him who rejoiceth and worketh righteousness, who remembereth thee in thy ways." (D&C 133:44.)

However, in spite of the Lord's efforts to keep us in remembrance of him, the scriptures repeatedly demonstrate "how quick the children of men do forget the Lord their God." (Alma 46:8.) There are many who do "not like to retain God in their knowledge," and who are "slow to remember the Lord their God. (See Romans 1:28; Mosiah 13:29.) "The wicked . . . will not seek after God: God is not in all his thoughts." (Psalms 10:4.) Mormon lamented over his people: "How slow are they to remember the Lord their God." He also sorrowed that in the best times of prosperity, "then is the time that they do harden their hearts, and do forget the Lord their God, and do trample under their feet the Holy One—yea, and this because of their ease, and their exceedingly great prosperity." (Helaman 12:5, 2.) One way to "trample" Christ under our feet is to take him for granted and allow other priorities to crowd him out of our thoughts and focus of attention. (See 1 Nephi 19:7.)

One reason keeping Christ focused in the center of our attention is so important is that the mind is very much like an electromagnet. It is as if our mind is polarized by the frequency and emotional intensity of the thoughts we hold in our attention, just as a bar of metal is polarized and magnetized when an electrical current is passed through it. Elder Dallin H. Oakes explained, "To remember means to keep in memory. In the scriptures, it often

means to keep a person in memory, together with associ-
ated emotions like love, loyalty, or gratitude. The stronger
the emotion, the more vivid and influential the memory."
(*Ensign*, May 1988, p. 29.) This attribute of the mind cre-
ates a law of mental function which is, "Whatever holds
your attention holds you." Pondering, contemplating or
holding Christ at the center of our thoughts and emotions
increases our love and appreciation for him.

Following his resurrection, Christ told the disciples in
America to "go ye unto your homes, and *ponder* upon the
things which I have said." (3 Nephi 17:3; emphasis added.)
This command was repeated in our own time. (See D&C
30:3.) It was while he sat in his room pondering the scriptures and the sacrifice Christ had made on our behalf that
President Joseph F. Smith received the great vision contained in Section 138 of the Doctrine and Covenants. And
it was following deep meditation on the scriptures pertaining to the resurrection and the rewards that follow it that
Joseph Smith and Sidney Rigdon received the inspiring,
unparalleled revelations in Section 76. Meditating, pondering, and contemplating the majesty of Christ and the
things he has done for us will always "magnetize" our
minds, as it were, and attract the spiritual experiences
that lead to closer fellowship with him.

This is why the Savior asked us to participate in the
ordinance of the Sacrament frequently. The Lord
expressed a spiritual formula concerning this principle in
the Sacrament prayers, wherein we witness to the Father
that we are not only "willing to take upon [us] the name"
of Christ, but also that we will "always remember him and
keep his commandments." (D&C 20:77.) Because the
scriptures emphasize that we always reap what we sow,
the logical reward for holding Christ in our thoughts is
"that [we] may always have his Spirit to be with [us]."
(D&C 20:77.) Isn't that exactly what we need to achieve if
we are to know him personally and feel close to him?

Just as the strength of that electromagnet is dependent upon or proportionate to the amount of current
passed through the bar of metal, so it is with us spiritually. The more we hold Christ in our thoughts, the more we
will have his Spirit to be with us. It is like a mathematical

ratio. The more we learn to hold him in the focus of our attention, the closer we will feel to him and the more prepared we will be to receive his personal fellowship. "What holds your attention holds you." The problem is that sometimes we are so busy trying to remember and obey a seemingly endless list of commandments and duties, that we miss the power key in the sacrament: remembering *him*; remembering the person of Jesus Christ and all that he has done for us.

The reverse of the ratio is also true. The less we focus upon Christ and his scriptural promises, the farther away he will seem. The less we think about him, the more room there will be for the problems, temptations and distractions of the world to crowd into our minds and separate us from the Savior and the fellowship he is seeking to give us. King Benjamin verified that if we would be close to Christ, "Ye should remember to retain [his] name written always in your hearts, that ye are not found on the left hand of God, but that ye hear and know the voice by which ye shall be called . . . For how knoweth a man the master . . . who is a stranger unto him, and is far from the thoughts and intents of his heart? (Mosiah 5:12-13.) We can't expect to make a personal friend of someone we hardly ever think about except for a few minutes once a week in church.

Christ has commanded us to "Look unto me in every thought." (D&C 6:36.) To obey this commandment requires practice and determination. One might wonder if this is even possible, considering the demands of work, school, parenting, housekeeping and all the other things that demand our attention. One of Satan's greatest efforts is to draw our thoughts and attention away from the Lord. However, with the assistance of the Holy Spirit, it is quite possible for those who truly desire his companionship to remember him in their daily thoughts. Remembering the Lord always is a skill that grows with practice. We simply start from where we are, sharing our desire with the Lord and asking for his help in remembering him. Consider the entire verse: Steven (insert your name) "Look unto me in every thought; [and Steven,] doubt not, fear not." (D&C 6:36.) In other words, don't let Satan fill your minds with doubts about his love or his power to change your life, doubts about his willingness to be close to you. Don't be afraid to seek his fellowship. He will respond by drawing near to you and bringing the reality of his love into your heart.

One of the things we must each do before we can experience this closeness to Christ and Heavenly Father is to remove the unworthy thoughts that Satan and the world try so hard to plant in our consciousness. The Savior has specified exactly how we go about gaining confidence in his presence. "Let virtue garnish thy thoughts unceasingly," he said, and "then shall thy confidence wax strong in the presence of God." (D&C 121:45.) We cannot have confidence in his presence, nor can we have confidence in our prayers while we deliberately indulge unworthy thoughts, whether they are thoughts of an immoral nature, or thoughts of unkind feelings toward someone we need to forgive. "If I regard iniquity in my heart, the Lord will not hear me." (Psalms 66:18.) We cannot deliberately allow or indulge unworthy thoughts and expect to draw close to him, because "the Spirit of the Lord doth not dwell in unholy temples." (Helaman 4:24.) We can show the Lord that we do not "regard" or contemplate the pleasures of unworthy thoughts by resolving to let no picture hang on the walls of our imagination that we would not hang on the walls of our home.

In addition to purifying our thoughts, there are two very simple things we can do to remind ourselves to think about the Savior more often. The first is to place your favorite picture of him where you will see it often. The second thing we can do is to take a 3x5 card and print six words on it. The six words are: I AM A DISCIPLE OF CHRIST. This simple affirmation will change the way you think about yourself and the way you think about Jesus Christ. Take this card with you everywhere you go and refer to it frequently throughout the day. Remember the principle: "What holds your attention holds you," which has the same meaning as: "For as he thinketh in his heart, so is he." Or as phrased in the sacrament prayer, by remembering him always, we will "always have his Spirit to be with us."

Carry the 3x5 card in your pocket or purse and make it a habit to read it several times a day. Repeat the affirmation frequently, even when you are not looking at the card. Many people make extra cards to tape on their bathroom mirrors, on the refrigerator, or over the kitchen sink—anywhere they will be seen often.

"I AM A DISCIPLE OF CHRIST" is a very powerful affirmation. We simply cannot read that commitment several times a day and then deliberately do things that a disciple wouldn't do. After using this card long enough to repolarize your mind by focusing on the Savior, you will find your thought process changing. When faced with temptations that you might previously have wanted to give in to, your mind will object: "Wait a minute, a disciple of Christ wouldn't do that." President David O. McKay said, "I never make a decision without asking myself, How will I explain this to the Savior when I meet him?" (See *Ensign*, August 1984, p. 38.) After using this affirmation or commitment card for several days, you will find, when you are faced with decisions and choices, your mind will automatically guide you into the question, "What would a disciple of Christ do?"

So by choosing to train our minds to remember the Savior, and then walking the path that a true disciple walks, we will find him walking with us, closer than we ever dreamed would be possible. We will be able to say, "I meditate on all thy works," and "I remember thee upon my bed, and meditate on thee in the night watches." (Psalms 143:5; 63:6.) We will be able to invite the Lord to "Consider my meditation," and to pray with confidence that "the meditation of my heart be acceptable in thy sight, O Lord, my strength, and my redeemer." (Psalms 5:1; 19:14.)

Steven (insert your name) "Cry unto God for all thy support; yea, let all thy doings be unto the Lord, and [Steven,] whithersoever thou goest let it be in the Lord; yea, let all thy thoughts be directed unto the Lord; yea, let the affections of thy heart be placed upon the Lord forever." (Alma 37:36.)

Growing Closer Through the Scriptures

The next key to making friends with the Savior is to make friends of his scriptures. The more time we spend with the scriptures, the more time we will spend with him. To our minds and hearts, searching the scriptures is like the electricity we talked about passing through the bar of metal to magnetize and polarize it. If there is no current, there will be no magnetism, no power. Pondering the Savior's revealed words, especially the Book of Mormon, is the most direct route to purifying our thoughts and enriching our prayer life. The more time we invest in the scriptures, the less trouble we will have with our thoughts. The scriptures are the fastest, most direct path I have found to knowing and loving the Savior and our Heavenly Father. It is the essential foundation to preparing to meet them face to face.

Before we discuss this key further, I want to share excerpts with you from two letters I have in my possession. The first is from a woman who was in suicidal despair because of loneliness and what she perceived to be stony, silent heavens. Captive to life-long addictions which she could not overcome, she wrote:

> Brother Cramer, to be blunt, I find it very difficult to believe what you say about faith in Christ. Over the years I've prayed and fasted and set goals till I was blue in the face. Nothing every happened for real progress or deep, internal changes in my life.

I've heard others testify of being healed of addictions to drugs, alcohol, etc, but I can't believe it anymore because I have personally asked Christ to help me and nothing has happened.

I'm just left feeling alone. I ask myself time and again, how much more will I have to suffer? Doesn't the Lord know my feelings, my pain and anguish? Doesn't he care?

What did you feel while reading this letter? Didn't your heart identify with her distress? Think about this: you don't even know her, yet you had feelings of compassion. Right? But wait a minute. You do know her, at least in part, because she has just opened her heart to you. And if you could read the rest of her letter, you would know even more about her. Now let me share part of another letter:

Something strange and beautiful and powerful is happening within me. I can't explain what I'm feeling, except that I feel a sense of peace and power and confidence I have never known before.

Even though I don't understand all of this, it doesn't matter. The fact is that I know it is true and I can actually feel my heart changing. Now I realize how blind I've been all these years in thinking I had to be perfect and do everything just right before Christ would help me or accept me.

I've been in the way of his healing. It wasn't that he wasn't willing or able to help me. I just wasn't willing to get out of the way with my stubborn pride and false ideas. He's been there all the time, pleading and striving to draw me to him and I wouldn't let him.

What a beautiful testimony! The second letter is from the same woman, after only three months of intense scripture study. And just as these few short paragraphs enabled you to know a lot about this wonderful woman, even so the scriptures reveal the Lord's personality; his likes and dislikes; how he feels about things, and what he wants us to do in our lives.

In order to feel comfortable with myself, I must get to know myself as God reveals me in the scriptures.

In order to feel comfortable with God, I must get to know God as he reveals himself in the scriptures. (Don Baker, *Acceptance*, Portland, Oregon: Multnomah Press, 1985, p. 122.)

Now consider two more letters. The first one reads, "Some of you are guilty before me, but I will be merciful unto your weakness." The second one says, "I will that ye should overcome the world; wherefore I will have compassion upon you." These two letters are addressed directly to us. They are from our elder brother, Jesus Christ. The full text is in Doctrine and Covenants, Sections 38 and 64. What do they teach about the Savior? They both reveal parts of the Lord's divine personality that make it easier for us to approach him. The scriptures are full of such self-revelation: "The scriptures teach us how the Father has related to his children in the past; more important, they teach us how he will relate to us if we are worthy and if we seek him." (Mollie H. Sorensen, "Learning Faith," *Ensign*, March 1985, p. 27.)

The point is that we cannot know Christ or Heavenly Father without searching and pondering the words they have given us in the scriptures. Jesus Christ feels so strongly about this that he actually equates our feelings toward the scriptures to our feelings toward him and Heavenly Father. He said, "If a man love me, he will keep my words." (John 14:23.) Or personalized: "Steven, [insert your name] if you love me, you will keep my words." "Keeping" his words means more than obedience to his commandments. It also means keeping them focused in our thoughts. How could we possibly claim to love him if we do not "keep" his words focused in our conscious minds? "If a man love me, he will keep my words." Would we call him a liar by claiming to love him while we treat his words with casual indifference and make little effort to learn and remember them? "For where your treasure is, there will your heart be also." (Matthew 6:21.)

The entire passage reads: "If a man (or woman) love me, he will keep my words: and my Father will love him, and we will come unto him, and make our abode with him. [But] he that loveth me not keepeth not my sayings." (John 14:23-24.) We have another spiritual formula here, just as we found in the memory covenant of the sacrament prayers. This formula is: "love of scripture = love of Christ, and indifference to scripture = indifference toward the Savior and Heavenly Father." Perhaps that sounds harsh, but the Savior was teaching that neither he nor the Father will ever become familiar to us until we are familiar with their recorded words. "Wherefore, ye must press forward . . . feasting upon the word of Christ," for his words "shall not depart out of thy mouth; but thou shalt meditate therein day and night." (2 Nephi 31:20; Joshua 1:8.)

Jesus also said, "Whoso receiveth not my voice is not acquainted with my voice, and is not of me," but "whosoever [does receive] my word receiveth me." (D&C 84:52; 112:20.) Again it is a mathematical ratio: the more time we spend reading and pondering his letters to us, as it were, the more intimately we will know him, the more we will love and appreciate him, and the quicker we will be prepared to meet him. As a word of caution, I want to say that even something as noble and spiritual as reading the scriptures can become an obsession. We must use caution not to substitute reading scriptures for all the other good things he expects us to do; we need to not only read the scriptures but act on them also: "Blessed are they that hear the word of God, and keep it," for "whoso keepeth his word, in him verily is the love of God perfected: hereby know we that we are in him." (Luke 11:28; 1 John 2:5.)

And I now give unto you a commandment to beware concerning yourselves, to give diligent heed to the words of eternal life.

For you shall live by every word that proceedeth forth from the mouth of God. (D&C 84:43-44.)

We cannot possibly "live by his every word" unless we give them "diligent heed" and learn to treasure these self-revelations as glimpses into the divine personality. The will of the Lord and the word of the Lord are one and the same. How can we know the will of God for us unless we know the word of God? How can we place Christ at the center of our lives if we are ignorant of his word? How can we rely upon the Lord for strength and guidance in time of need if we do not know how loving and caring he is, if we do not know specifically what he has promised, in his scriptures, to do for us? Surely that is why Christ said that "you must rely upon my word." (D&C 17:1.)

"These words are not of men nor of man," said the Savior, "for it is my voice which speaketh them unto you . . . and by my power you can read them . . . wherefore," when you have read my words from the scripture, you can actually "testify that you have heard my voice, and know my words." (D&C 18:34-36.) When we study and meditate on the scriptures, it is much the same as coming into the presence of God. Indeed, when our scriptural study is accompanied by the Holy Ghost we will know and feel that we have been touched by the influence and presence of the Lord in a very real way. Job set the standard when he said, "I have esteemed the words of his mouth more than my necessary food." (Job 23:12.)

> Search the scriptures; for . . . they are they which testify of me. (John 5:39.)

> And now, (Steven—insert your name) remember the words of him who is the life and light of the world, your Redeemer, your Lord and your God. (D&C 10:70.)

> I will delight myself in thy statutes: I will not forget thy word. (Psalms 119:16.)

Growing Closer
Through Service

Our relationship with Christ is dependent upon our service in his cause of saving and exalting his brothers and sisters. As long as we wisely keep our lives in balance, the more we serve him, the better we will know him and the closer we will feel. The more indifferent we are to his cause, the less time and emotion we invest in his service, the more distant he will seem. Or, as Elder Taylor stated "The greater your service, the closer your access to God." (Elder Russell C. Taylor, *Ensign*, November 1984, pp. 23-24.)

President Gordon B. Hinckley stated, "There can be no true worship of Christ without giving of ourselves." (*Ensign*, March 1987, p. 5.) Jesus said, "Choose ye this day, to serve the Lord God who made you," because "If thou lovest me thou shalt serve me." (Moses 6:33; D&C 42:29.) Converts in Book of Mormon times were not "received unto baptism save they took upon them the name of Christ, having a determination to serve him to the end." (Moroni 6:3.) Baptism was considered "a testimony that ye have entered into a covenant to serve him until you are dead." (Mosiah 18:13.) The same is true of our baptismal covenants today. Membership in Christ's church requires not only repentance of our sins, but also that we "are willing to take upon [us] the name of Jesus Christ, having a determination to serve him to the end." (D&C 20:37.) It is through this devoted, serving discipleship that Christ is working to "raise up unto myself a pure people, that will serve me in righteousness." (D&C 100:16.)

It is impossible to demonstrate our love for God without service to our brothers and sisters. Even the "golden rule" is based on service. "All things whatsoever ye would that men should do to you, do ye even so to them." (Matthew 7:12.) Thus we are commanded to "Strengthen ye the weak hands," to "Succor the weak, lift up the hands which hang down, and strengthen the feeble knees." (Isaiah 35:3; D&C 81:5.) As we seek to apply the golden rule we are told, Steven, (insert your name,) "remember in all things the poor and the needy, the sick and the afflicted, for [Steven,] he that doeth not these things, the same is not my disciple." (D&C 52:40.) "Service is an imperative for those who worship Jesus Christ." (Elder Dallin H. Oaks, *Ensign*, November 1984, p. 12.) One of the ways Jesus Christ will "discern between the righteous and the wicked," will be by distinguishing "between him that serveth God and him that serveth him not." (3 Nephi 24:18.)

It is a joy to serve Christ when we feel appreciation for all he has given us. "Only fear the Lord, and serve him in truth with all your heart: for consider how great things he hath done for you." (1 Samuel 12:24.) No one could possibly repay him in full, because even if we "should serve him with all [our] whole souls yet [we] would be unprofitable servants." (Mosiah 2:21.) But we must try to repay him and that is why "it is an imperative duty that we owe to all the rising generation . . . that we should waste and wear out our lives" in his service and "be not weary in well doing." (D&C 123:11-13; 2 Thessalonians 3:13.) Elder Russell C. Taylor said, "My experience teaches that the highest goodness attainable is a life of unselfish service to mankind. It has been wisely said, 'Service is the rent we pay for our own room on earth.' We should know that the rent is due on a daily basis and know that the receipt is never stamped 'paid in full,' because the rent, service in God's kingdom, is due today and due tomorrow." (*Ensign*, November 1984, p. 23.)

Unless we lose ourselves in the service of others, our lives are largely lived to no real purpose, for [Christ] went on to say, "He that loveth his life shall lose it; and he that hateth his life in this world shall keep it unto life eternal." (John 12:25.) Or, as recorded in Luke, "Whosoever shall seek to save his life shall lose it; and whosoever shall lose his life shall preserve it." (Luke 17:33.) In other words, he who lives only unto himself withers and dies, while he who forgets himself in the service of others grows and blossoms in this life and in eternity. (President Gordon B. Hinckley, *Ensign*, August 1982, p. 3.)

I heard a lovely song which said of Christ, "He went his quiet way, giving himself away." It reminded me of Acts 10:38 where Peter said Jesus "went about doing good," and the Savior's own words, "I am among you as he that serveth," for "The Son of man came not to be ministered unto, but to minister." (Luke 22:27; Matthew 20:28.) Having spent his life in selfless service, the Savior commanded his disciples to do the same thing. "For that which ye have seen me do even that shall ye do." (3 Nephi 27:21.) "For I have given you an example, that ye should do as I have done to you." (John 13:15.)

While serving others is vital, it is equally as important to take time to nourish ourselves. One of the examples Jesus set throughout his ministry was taking time out to rest and replenish his physical and spiritual reserves. "And see that all these things be done in wisom and order; it is not requisite that man should run faster than he has strength." (Mosiah 4:27; see also D&C 10:4)

Still, the Savior is ever searching for partners who will join him in the work of saving souls. It is sobering to know that he takes very personally how we treat our brothers and sisters. "Inasmuch as ye have done it unto the least of these my brethren, ye have done it unto me," he declared, but "Inasmuch as ye did it not to one of the least of these, ye did it not unto me." (Matthew 25:40, 45.)

One of my favorite true stories from the *Ensign* illustrates this point.

Many years ago in a small town in the southern part of Utah, my great grandmother was called to be the president of the Relief Society. During this period of our Church history there existed a very bitter and antagonistic spirit between the Mormons and the Gentiles.

In my great grandmother's ward, one of the young sisters married a gentile boy. This of course did not please either the Mormons or the Gentiles very much. In the course of time this young couple gave birth to a child. Unfortunately the mother became so ill in the process of childbirth that she was unable to care for her baby. Upon learning of this woman's condition, great grandmother immediately went to the homes of the sisters in the ward and asked them if they would take a turn going into the home of this young couple to care for the baby. One by one these women refused and so the responsibility fell completely upon her.

She would rise early in the morning, walk what was a considerable distance to the home of this young couple where she would bathe and feed the baby, gather all that needed to be laundered and take it with her to her home.

One morning she felt too weak and sick to go. However, as she lay in bed she realized that if she didn't go the child would not be provided for. [With the help of the Lord,] she mustered all her strength and went. [When she returned home, exhausted, she] collapsed into a large chair and immediately fell into a deep sleep. She said that as she slept she felt as if she were consumed by a fire that would melt the very marrow of her bones. She dreamed that she was bathing the Christ-Child and glorying in what a great privilege it would have been to have bathed the Son of God. Then the voice of the Lord spoke to her saying, "Inasmuch as ye have done it unto the least of these, ye have done it unto me." (Melchizedek Priesthood Manual, 1976-77, pp. 154-55 as quoted in *Ensign*, November 1981, p. 81.)

"He will measure our devotion to him by how we love and serve our fellowmen." (Elder Howard W. Hunter, *Ensign*, November 1986, p. 34.)

There are many people within our sphere of influence who are hungering and thirsting for the spiritual nourishment we could give them by leading their souls to Christ. There are people who feel like strangers to that bond of fellowship which the disciples of Christ enjoy; people who are sick at heart and imprisoned by weaknesses and bad habits they have not been able to conquer by themselves. They need us to teach them of the Savior's healing, liberating love. Spiritually they are naked and need our help to clothe themselves in the robes of righteousness so they will have the confidence to come to their Savior.

Steven, (insert your name) "When ye are in the service of your fellow beings, ye are only in the service of your God." (Mosiah 2:17.)

There are many rewards promised to disciples who give themselves to the Savior's cause. For example, Jesus said, "I, the Lord . . . delight to honor those who serve me in righteousness and in truth unto the end. Great shall be their reward and eternal shall be their glory." And "If any man serve me, him will my Father honour." (D&C 76:5-6; John 12:26.) Elder Jack H. Goaslind described another important benefit. "Service helps us forget our own travails; it enlarges our souls and gives us greater capacity to endure our own trials." (*Ensign*, May 1986, p. 54.) And President Gordon B. Hinckley said, "Generally speaking, the most miserable people I know are those who are obsessed with themselves; the happiest people I know are those who lose themselves in the service of others." (*Ensign*, August 1982, p. 5.)

But perhaps the greatest reward for serving the Master is the personal knowledge it brings of Jesus Christ. Just as the pioneer grandmother's selfless service allowed her to experience what it would be like to bathe the Christ-child, when we do the same things Jesus did, we are then privileged to feel what he felt. And by feeling the same emotions which Christ felt as he served, we come to know him and love him with greater devotion because we have become more like him. The truth of this principle is illustrated by the following portion of a letter from our daughter, Tracy, during her mission in Santiago, Chile.

In house after house, our investigators will break into tears, spilling out their problems to us. It's pretty scary to try and handle those situations if you don't have the Spirit, because you have no idea what to say. But it turns into a beautiful experience when the Spirit guides you.

I realized that people really do see us as servants of God. Otherwise, why would people pour out their deepest feelings, family and marital problems to us when we are young, single and inexperienced?

You'd think I'd go away depressed and burdened with everyone's problems. But every time I wipe their tears, every time I console an aching heart, every time I offer words of comfort, help them realize that God loves them, or give a prayer on their behalf, I feel more and more like Jesus Christ. And I walk away uplifted. It is a wonderful feeling, because I know the Lord is using me.

Elder Bruce R. McConkie stated, "If we are to know God we must believe as he believes, think as he thinks, and experience what he experiences." (*Ensign*, July 1972, p. 109.) King Benjamin challenged, "How knoweth a man the master whom he has not served, and who is a stranger unto him, and is far from the thoughts and intents of his heart?" And Elder Carlos E. Asay taught, "No one will ever know truly that Jesus is the Christ, and no one will ever fully understand the Savior's work until he has invested in the business of saving souls." (*Ensign*, October 1985, p. 50.)

To develop a close companionship with the Savior, we must first place him close to the desires and thoughts of our hearts. All that we do should be for the purpose of helping forward his work. (Relief Society Manual, 1982, p. 25.)

Growing Closer Through Prayer

Another key to knowing the Savior and feeling close to him is honest prayer to our Heavenly Father. Many people may wonder how they can develop a personal relationship with the Savior when they are only allowed to pray to Heavenly Father. Let me share three reasons why this can be accomplished.

One part of the answer is that Heavenly Father and the Savior work together as a team, along with the Holy Ghost, to lift us toward the light and glory they enjoy. When the Lord told Moses that "this is my work and my glory—to bring to pass the immortality and eternal life of man," it referred to the work of both the Father and the Son (Moses 1:39.) Elder Neal A. Maxwell said, "We cannot be close to one member of the Godhead without being close to all three." (*Notwithstanding My Weakness*, Salt Lake City, Utah: Deseret Book, 1981, p. 112.)

Another reason that sincere prayer to Heavenly Father brings us closer to Jesus Christ is that when we pray to the Father in the name of Jesus Christ, that prayer is heard and evaluated by Christ as well as the Father. Even though we do not pray to Jesus, he is just as aware of our prayers as if they had been directed to him personally. Consider some scriptures that illustrate this truth. "Thus saith the Lord your God, even Jesus Christ, the Great I AM . . . I have heard your prayers." (D&C 38:1, 16.) And again, "Behold, I, the Lord, who was crucified for the sins of the world . . . Behold, I say unto you, my servant Sidney Gilbert, that I have heard your prayers." (D&C 53:2, 1; see also 35:2-3.)

Verily thus saith the Lord unto you my servant Thomas: I have heard thy prayers; and thine alms have come up as a memorial before me . . .

I know thy heart, and have heard thy prayers . . .

Be faithful until I come, for I come quickly; and my reward is with me to recompense every man according as his work shall be. I am Alpha and Omega. (D&C 112:1, 11, 34.)

So when we pray to the Father, Jesus Christ is also listening and ready, under the direction of the Father, to do whatever is appropriate in response to our needs. For similar verses about the ears of our Savior's love, see D&C 21:7; 67:1-2; 96:6; 105:18-19. Brigham Young taught that one of "the greatest and most important of all requirements of our Father in Heaven is to . . . take a course to open and keep open a communication with your elder Brother, our Savior." (*Journal of Discourses*, Vol. 8, p. 339, as quoted in the 1982 Relief Society Manual, p. 24.) Many people wonder how they can "communicate" with their Savior and develop a personal relationship with him when they are only allowed to pray to Heavenly Father. Knowing that Christ also hears our prayers helps us to bridge that gap.

But there is another reason that sincere, honestly felt prayer to Heavenly Father brings us closer to Christ. After Heavenly Father has determined the proper response to our prayer, Jesus Christ is in charge of answering the prayer. Jesus Christ has three names that identify him as the one Father uses to answer our prayers. They are: "The Word, The Messenger of Salvation, and The Messenger of the Covenant." (See John 1:1-14; D&C 93:8; Mal. 3:1.) He is given these names to represent his mission to deliver the words, messages and revelations of the Father to his children on this earth. According to Elder Bruce R. McConkie, these three titles "signify that the words of salvation are in him; that he carries his Father's word to all men; that he is the executive and administrator who does the will of the Father; that the Father speaks and his word is executed by the Son. (See D&C 93:8.) The clear meaning is that God speaks his word, which the Son, by the power of the Spirit, puts into operation." (*Mormon Doctrine*, Salt Lake City, Utah: Bookcraft, 1966, p. 844.)

So, ever since mankind fell from the Father's presence in the Garden of Eden, Jesus Christ has functioned as the representative of the Father in delivering the revelations and answers to prayer that Father sends to his children on earth. There are many events in scriptural history which demonstrate this. For example, when the idolaters tied Abraham to their altar and prepared to take his life in sacrifice, he prayed to Heavenly Father for protection and deliverance. The one who answered for Heavenly Father was Jehovah, the premortal Christ. "And the Lord hearkened and heard, and he filled me with the vision of the Almighty . . . and immediately unloosed my bands; And his voice was unto me: Abraham, Abraham, behold, my name is Jehovah, and I have heard thee, and have come down to deliver thee." (Abraham 1:15-16.) Both the Father and the Son heard Abraham's prayer but Christ was sent to respond.

When Heavenly Father deemed it time to call Moses to lead Israel from Egyptian bondage he sent Jehovah, the premortal Christ to appear at the burning bush on Mount Sinai and instruct Moses in his duties. Moses asked the Lord's name so that he might tell Israel who it was that sent him. It was on this occasion that Jesus Christ identified himself as Jehovah, the God of "I AM THAT I AM," which declaration he repeated to the unbelieving Jews during his mortal mission and nearly caused him to be stoned for blasphemy. (See Exodus 3:14; John 8:57-58.) Knowing it was Jesus Christ instructing Moses for and in behalf of the Father brings meaning to his statement that I, Jehovah, or Jesus Christ, "have also heard the groaning of the children of Israel," and "I have surely seen the affliction of my people which are in Egypt, and have heard their cry by reason of their taskmasters; for I know their sorrows; And I am come down to deliver them." (Exodus 6:5; 3:7-8.) Once again, the people prayed to Heavenly Father and the Father's answer to their prayers was implemented by Jesus Christ, the Savior and Shepherd of this world.

We see yet another example in the brother of Jared's request to Heavenly Father to illuminate sixteen stones so they might have light inside their ships. "O Lord," he prayed to Heavenly Father, "thou hast given us a commandment that we must call upon thee, that from thee we may receive according to our desires. And I know, O Lord, that thou hast all power, and can do whatsoever thou wilt for the benefit of man; therefore touch these stones, O Lord, with thy finger, and prepare them that they may shine forth in darkness." (Ether 3:2, 4.)

In answer to this prayer, Jesus Christ was sent to fulfill the Father's will. "And it came to pass that when the brother of Jared had said these words, behold, the Lord (Jesus Christ) stretched forth his hand and touched the stones one by one with his finger. And the veil was taken from off the eyes of the brother of Jared, and he saw the finger of the Lord." (Ether 3:6.) We know it was *Christ's* spiritual finger that he saw, because in response to the brother of Jared's faith, the Savior then stepped through the veil and allowed him to behold his entire spirit body, saying, "Behold, I am he who was prepared from the foundation of the world to redeem my people. Behold, I am Jesus Christ." (Ether 3:14.)

Centuries later, just before the Savior's mortal birth, the disciples in America were under threat of death if the prophesied signs did not appear. Fearing for the lives of the believers, Nephi prayed earnestly to Heavenly Father for help. In response to that prayer it was Jesus Christ himself who delivered the answer: "Lift up your head and be of good cheer; for behold, the time is at hand, and on this night shall the sign be given, and on the morrow come I into the world." (3 Nephi 1:13.)

And finally, when Joseph Smith prayed to Heavenly Father in the Sacred Grove both the Father and the Son appeared, but it was Jesus Christ who answered the questions and provided the instructions for the boy prophet. "This is My Beloved Son. Hear Him!" was all the Father said. (Joseph Smith—History 1:17.)

So we see that the Savior's ears are lovingly attuned to our needs and desires in conjunction with the Father's. However, we must not let the knowledge that Christ is the one who executes the answers to our prayers lead us into the folly that is common throughout Christianity: the mistake of praying directly to Jesus instead of to the Father. We note that whenever Christ has given instructions about prayer, he has carefully emphasized that it is not to him that we should pray, but to the Father. "After this manner therefore pray ye: Our Father which art in heaven." (Matthew 6:9; see also 3 Nephi 13:9.) And again, "Ye must always pray unto the Father in my name." (3 Nephi 18:19; see also D&C 42:3; 88:64.)

The Savior has also stressed that even though he is the one implementing the answer to our prayers, they are not his answers, but the Father's. "I am come in my Father's name," and "My doctrine is not mine, but his that sent me." (John 5:43; 7:16.) Christ has carefully taught that he does nothing on our behalf except as directed by the Father. (See John 5:19; 8:28.)

If you weren't aware that Christ is involved in answering our prayers, consider one of Alma's prophecies about the coming of Christ, when he said, "And not many days hence the Son of God shall come in his glory; and his glory shall be the glory of the Only Begotten of the Father, full of grace, equity, and truth, full of patience, mercy, and longsuffering, quick to hear the cries of his people and to answer their prayers." (Alma 9:26.) President Benson verified Alma's message when he encouraged us to, "Establish a deep and abiding relationship with the Lord Jesus Christ. Know that he is there—always there. Reach out to him. He does answer prayers." (*Ensign*, November 1988, p.97.)

Because of his love for each individual, the Savior's ears are always attentive to our cries for help. During his mortal ministry, it was not uncommon for Christ to be followed by huge crowds, often as large as three to five thousand men plus the accompanying women and children. One can easily imagine the great noise that would attend such crowds, and yet the Savior's ears of love were always attuned to the one most in need. When he came down from the Mount of Transfiguration, the Savior was met by many crying for his attention, but out of the entire crowd, the one he heard first was the father whose child was subject to violent seizures. (See Luke 9:37-41.)

As the Savior approached the city of Jericho, he was again followed by a great multitude. We can imagine how they clamored for his attention, but above all that noise, the ears of his love were able to hear the cry of one not even a part of the group. It came from a blind man named Bartimaeus who "sat by the way side, begging." When Bartimaeus heard the noise of the multitude he asked the cause. Learning that it was Jesus they followed, he cried out to the Master. And that plea for help pierced through the noise of the crowd into the sensitive, discerning ears of the Savior. To the amazement of the multitudes, "Jesus stood still, and commanded him to be called." A murmur of curiosity must have rippled through the crowd as they inquired the cause of the delay in the journey. Why had he stopped? Why was he so still? What had captured his attention? "What wilt thou that I should do unto thee?" he asked of the one whose cry for help had reached him in spite of the noise of the crowd. "Lord, that I might receive my sight. And Jesus said unto him, Go thy way; thy faith hath made thee whole. And immediately he received his sight, and followed Jesus in the way." (Matthew 20:29-34; Mark 10:46-52; Luke 18:35-43.)

There was a time of darkness in my own life when I, too, was blind, not physically, but spiritually. In deep remorse and shame for past mistakes, I resolved to abandon my entanglements and find my way back. However, I was blinded by hopelessness and self-loathing. On the very first day of my decision to repent I wavered and crumbled under Satan's pressure to return to my sins. I wanted to make things right with the Lord and my family, but I was afraid and lacked the strength to remain firm. That night, afraid to go home and confess, I paced back and forth on a canal bank where I could be alone. I sobbed. I wrestled. I needed to pray, but how could I after the sinful choices I had made?

"You are not worthy to pray," Satan shouted at me gleefully. "You have no right to pray." I guess that's true, I reasoned. What right do I have to expect God to hear my prayer now, after what I've done? I didn't know the love and mercy of a Heavenly Father and Savior who had waited for years for this moment to come. I didn't know that every child of God has the right to call to his Father in Heaven, no matter what he has done. Nothing can take that right away. I didn't know that nothing will stop the Lord from hearing a sincere prayer, not even our sins.

When I felt I could stand it no longer, an involuntary prayer escaped my lips, the first I had uttered in many, many months. "It's too hard," I cried, weeping with fear and weakness. "I can't do this by myself." And then, like a gusher, all the heartache and shame poured out and I wept, totally confessing.

The moment I finished my tormented plea, in that very instant the Lord's answer was there. The ears of his love were just waiting for this prayer and instantly his voice was in my mind, reassuring me that I was not alone. His peace encompassed me and soothed my fears, witnessing that he had heard my cry and that I was loved. Loved? Yes! Loved no less than before. The message was as clear and unmistakable as if he had appeared before my eyes. There was absolutely no doubt that he had heard my prayer. I was stunned, overwhelmed by this unexpected response.

> But verily God hath heard me; he hath attended to the voice of my prayer. Blessed be God, which hath not turned away my prayer, nor his mercy from me. (Psalms 66:19-20.)

> Steven, (insert your name,) "He will be very gracious unto thee at the voice of thy cry; [and Steven,] when he shall hear it, he will answer thee." (Isaiah 30:19.)

> And in the time of their trouble, when they cried unto thee, thou heardst them from heaven . . . according to thy manifold mercies. (Nehemiah 9:27.)

So now we know that there is nothing we can do or say or feel or need or pray about without the notice and response of both Christ and the Father, who are united as a team to bring us back into their presence. Yet we are reluctant to pray about many situations and feelings. This we must overcome. If we would be close to Christ and Heavenly Father, we must hold nothing secret from them. Nothing. Bishop H. Burke Peterson teaches that we should make our prayers to Heavenly Father a practice in honest expression of our deepest feelings and desires.

> As you feel the need to confide in the Lord or to improve the quality of your visits with him, may I suggest a process to follow: go where you can be alone, go where you can speak out loud to him. The bedroom, the bathroom, or the closet will do.
> Now, picture him in your mind's eye. Think to whom you are speaking. Control your thoughts, don't let them wander. Address him as your Father and your friend.
> Now tell him things you really feel to tell him. Not trite phrases that have little meaning, but have a sincere, heartfelt conversation with him. Confide in him, thank him, ask him for forgiveness, plead with him, enjoy him, express your love to him, and then listen for his answers. (Melchizedek Priesthood Manual, 1974-75, p. 117.)

Sometimes we are reluctant to have that honest, open, heartfelt conversation because we are ashamed of our evil, selfish or unworthy desires. At other times we are reluctant to express our deepest desires or concerns because of the doubts which fill our minds. Doubts such as "I'm not worthy of such a request. After all I have done, he would never listen to me." Or, "God is much too busy to get involved in such a small matter. I don't dare ask such a thing of God." And finally, and perhaps the most tragic doubt of all, "Who do I think I am to bother God with such a request?" The truth is that honest prayers never bother him. The way we do bother him is by avoiding prayer, or by going through the motions but refusing to honestly, frankly discuss our desires and problems. "Have mercy upon me, O Lord, for I am in trouble." (Psalms 31:9.)

Since both Heavenly Father and the Savior "comprehendeth all things," and because "all things are naked and opened unto the eyes of him with whom we have to do," and because "the Lord searcheth all hearts, and understandeth all the imagination of the thoughts," it should come as no surprise that God is always aware of our desires, even before we have expressed them to him. (See D&C 88:41; Hebrews 4:13; 1 Chronicles 28:9.)

> For [Steven, insert your name] your Father knoweth what things ye have need of before ye ask him. (3 Nephi 13:8.)

When we pray, there is no use pretending. Like it or not, God knows us better than we know ourselves. Since God already knows what we feel, desire and need, and since we can never hide anything from him or surprise him with a need he hasn't already anticipated, doesn't it make sense to go ahead and express ourselves honestly?

We wouldn't be ashamed to go to our medical doctor with a fever or a rash. Why should we be ashamed to go to our Heavenly Father when we need spiritual help? It is Satan who wants to delay our prayers until after we are feeling clean and worthy. He knows that if we do not pray in our need, we will remain in our need. The medical doctor doesn't look down on us for coming to him with a problem. Rather, he is happy with the opportunity to help restore our health. He respects us for caring enough about our health to take the appropriate action. And the Lord, in his divine perfection and love, is delighted when we trust him enough to share our problems and deepest feelings.

One more principle to remember about the ears of our Father and Savior's love is our privilege of pleading for a response. We know, because of their perfection, that it would be impossible to utter a prayer that went unheard. But in those times when it seems the heavens are silent, we have the right and privilege to plead, as did Joseph, "O Lord God Almighty, hear us in these our petitions, and answer us from heaven . . . O hear, O hear, O hear us, O Lord! And answer these petitions." (D&C 109:77-78; see also Daniel 9:19.) The Lord is not offended when we plead, "Let thine ear be inclined; let thine heart be softened, and thy bowels moved with compassion toward us." (D&C 121:4.)

Asking Father to hear our prayers, however, does not give us the right to demand that he answer on our timetable. The spiritually mature person will exercise patience and trust, knowing that Father will respond in the divine timing that will be for our best good, remembering his promise to "order all things for your good, as fast as ye are able to receive them." (D&C 111:11.) Nevertheless, when circumstances are pressing upon us and the need is urgent, we may pray with humble and submissive hearts, "Lord, I cry unto thee: make haste unto me; give ear unto my voice, when I cry unto thee." (Psalms 141:1.)

Knowing that both the Father and the Savior are there, listening intently with ears of love, helps us to endure the times when they are silent because there is more that we must learn or experience before we receive the desired answer.

There is nothing too trivial to discuss with our Heavenly Father. When we are honest in our prayers, concealing nothing, those very problems which used to separate us from God will now draw us closer to both the Father and the Son, and prepare us for the day we meet them face to face.

I waited patiently for the Lord: and he inclined unto me, and heard my cry. (Psalms 40:1.)

Evening, and morning, and at noon, will I pray, and cry aloud: and he shall hear my voice. (Psalms 55:17.)

Growing Closer
By Forgiving

If we would draw closer to the Savior, we must learn to forgive those who have hurt us, as well as forgiving ourselves for past mistakes. The Savior can overlook many imperfections in those who draw near to him, but refusing to forgive erects almost impenetrable barriers between us and the Lord.

FORGIVING ONESELF

In the chapter entitled "The Arms of Forgiveness," we discussed the Savior's eagerness to forgive and remove the effects of every repented sin. But some of us get so trapped by our guilt and shame that we just can't let go of it and believe in the forgiveness Christ is trying to give us. Instead of surrendering our guilt to the Savior, we cling to it like a prisoner's ball and chain, dragging the past and our guilt with us everywhere we go.

Many times our perpetual self-condemnation is like setting up a mental video that never stops. Over and over it replays our painful past and we sink lower and lower into despair and self-loathing. What an offense to a magnificent, forgiving Savior when we insist on clinging to the past and condemning ourselves after Christ has accepted our repentance. The loving forgiveness of our Savior can turn that video replay off. It can stop the cycles of self-condemnation, if we will only accept it and stop punishing ourselves. The Savior is anxious to forgive us, but he will not force it upon

us. We must open our hearts to it. Elder Neal A. Maxwell
has counselled, "Some of us who would not chastise a
neighbor for his frailties have a field day with our own. We
should, of course, learn from our mistakes, but without forever studying the instant replays as if these were the game
of life itself." (*Ensign*, November 1976, pp. 13-14.)

The problem for many of us is that it is easier to perse-
cute ourselves than it is to humble ourselves by relying
upon the Savior's mercy and forgiveness. Such a preoccupation with past mistakes locks in guilt and locks out
forgiveness. We think we are being crushed by the demands
of justice when it is only our own failure to take advantage
of the atonement as it applies to our personal sins. We simply cannot hasten our salvation by self-punishment and
self-condemnation. Trying to do so only puts barriers
between us and the healing atonement of Jesus Christ.

Elder Richard G. Scott also commented on those who
cannot forgive themselves for past transgressions, even
when they know the Lord has forgiven them. He stressed
that "suffering does not bring forgiveness. It comes
through faith in Christ and obedience to his teachings, so
that his gift of redemption can apply." He continued:
"Can't you see that to continue to suffer for sins, when
there has been proper repentance and forgiveness of the
Lord, is not prompted by the Savior but by the master of
deceit, whose goal has always been to bind and enslave
the children of our Father in Heaven? Satan would
encourage you to continue to relive the details of past
mistakes, knowing that such thoughts make progress,
growth, and service difficult to attain." (*Ensign*, May
1986, pp. 10-11.)

The Lord has commanded us to forgive: Steven, (insert
your name,) "I, the Lord, will forgive whom I will forgive,
but [Steven,] of you it is required to forgive all men."
(D&C 64:10.)

Elder Theodore M. Burton stressed that forgiving "all
men" includes forgiving ourselves. "I find here an answer,"
he said, "for some who refuse to forgive themselves and
who make themselves miserable by continually talking
about their sins. They say, 'I just can't forgive myself for
the things I have done.' I reply, 'Do you think you are
more holy than the Lord? If He is willing to forgive you,

shouldn't you be willing to forgive yourself now that you have repented of your sin?' " (*Ensign*, June 1987, p. 15.)

So what we are saying is that by slightly twisting and distorting our well-intended feelings of remorse, Satan cleverly redirects our course away from God so that we find ourselves prisoners, held hostage by his diabolical distortion that the more guilty we feel, the more repentant and holy we are! By clinging to our guilt after repentance, we are not only rejecting the Savior's forgiveness, we are, in effect, saying to God, "Look at me Heavenly Father. See how angry I am with myself over my weaknesses and sins. Do you see how miserable I am making myself to please you?" What an awful distortion and tragedy. There is no way a person can develop a close relationship with deity when they believe such lies.

How can we know if our guilt feelings are healthy or harmful? How can we be sure if they are appropriate or inappropriate? The way to tell is incredibly simple. *True guilt* moves us to repentance and pulls us back to God, while *false guilt*, the distorted, over emphasized, self-condemning guilt, pulls us down and builds barriers between us and God.

FORGIVING OTHERS

If we would be close to the Lord, we must not only accept the forgiveness he offers us, but we must also give it freely to those who have hurt us. Speaking to those who desire a closer relationship with him, the Savior said, "If ye shall come unto me, [Steven—insert your name] or shall desire to come unto me, and rememberest that thy brother hath aught against thee—go thy way unto thy brother, and first be reconciled to thy brother, and then come unto me with full purpose of heart, and [Steven,] I will receive you." (3 Nephi 12:23-24.) H. Burke Peterson, of the Presiding Bishopric said that "No one can be classed as a true follower of the Savior who is not in the process of removing from his heart and mind every feeling of ill will, bitterness, hatred, envy, or jealousy toward another." (*Ensign*, November 1983, p. 60.)

The Savior has indicated that he welcomes those who seek his fellowship, promising that if we seek to draw near to him, he will respond by drawing near to us. (See D&C

88:63.) But he has established the prerequisite that we must first cleanse our hearts and interpersonal relationships of all feelings of bitterness and resentment. "I, the Lord, will forgive whom I will forgive, but of you it is required to forgive all men." (D&C 64:10.) One thing that helps to maintain a compassionate, forgiving attitude toward others is to imagine how terrible you would feel if you went to the Lord for forgiveness and he responded in a hesitant or negative manner as we sometimes do with each other. That is very sobering. So are these words: "If ye forgive men their trespasses, your heavenly Father will also forgive you. But if ye do not forgive, neither will your Father which is in heaven forgive your trespasses." (Matthew 6:14; Mark 11:26.)

Elder Theodore M. Burton said, "It is wicked to reject a child of God simply because he made an error. We need not be tolerant of the sin, but we must become tolerant and forgiving of the sinner." (*Ensign*, May 1983, p. 71.) Forgiving the offender does not mean we are condoning his sins. By forgiving we are not agreeing with the offense. We are only showing that the person who hurt us is more important than the mistake he made. True forgiveness is letting go of the injury without trying to correct the wrong.

Someone said, "Forgiveness is giving up my right to hurt you for hurting me." Refusing to forgive shows that we are more interested in having someone to blame than we are in letting go of the hurt and becoming closer to the Savior. If any person ever had the right to blame and withhold forgiveness, it was the crucified Christ. I am inspired by the words of the hymn: "Although in agony he hung, no murmuring word escaped his tongue." (*LDS Hymns*, 1985, p. 191.) What right do we have to judge, condemn, or withhold forgiveness for the petty injustices done to us, when compared to what Christ suffered and forgave?

The Savior warned, "He that forgiveth not his brother his trespasses standeth condemned before the Lord; for there remaineth in him the greater sin." (D&C 64:9.) Suppose a person breaks his marriage vows and commits adultery and the spouse refuses to forgive. Who did the Lord say committed the greater sin? Discussing how this scripture applies to our attitude toward major transgressions, Elder Theodore M. Burton said, "I take that to mean that it is a greater sin to refuse to forgive a person than it is to commit the sin for which that person was disfellow-shipped or excommunicated." (*Ensign*, May 1983, p. 72.)

But what if that person is not repentant? What if this person says, "I did it and I'm glad. I'll probably do it again." What then? The answer is unchanged. "I, the Lord, will forgive whom I will forgive, but of you it is required to forgive all men." (D&C 64:10.) How many of us would have the slightest chance of salvation if it weren't for Christ's sacrifice and atonement? Who of us can claim celestial glory without the mercy and forgiveness of our Savior, who stands before justice to cancel the debt of our personal sins? Because none of us are without sin, we all need forgiveness.

When the scriptures instruct us to forgive each other freely, nothing is said of who is right or who is wrong, only that we must forgive, whether the other party is repentant or not. A common error is in feeling that we do not have to forgive until the offender admits their error and asks for our forgiveness. Another error is in telling ourselves that we will forgive, but the one who hurt us will have to make the first move. Such feelings are unworthy of the disciple of Christ who seeks to draw close to the Lord. To be right with our Savior, we must forgive without regard to the offender's humility or lack of it, without regard to their repentance or lack of it.

Sometimes our forgiveness will end their sin. However, many times the hurtful behavior will continue, mocking our forgiveness. But because we have followed the Savior by forgiving, we will be given the strength to bear the burden and also the compassion to feel love toward the offender. There is no other way. We simply cannot be close to the Lord when we refuse to surrender unkind feelings toward someone who has wronged us.

Speaking of how we should deal with those who continue to hurt us or refuse to repent of past offenses, the Lord said, "Ye ought to say in your hearts—let God judge between me and thee, and reward thee according to thy deeds." (D&C 64:11.) That may sound like a curse, but it is not. There is great healing when we let go of the pain, when we refuse to punish the offender, when we surrender the injustice to him who suffered the greatest injustice of all. Leaving the judgment of the offender to the Lord is the path to freedom and peace, even though the offense may not be righted. Would we be close to the Lord? Forgiving others is the price.

Sometimes we think we are doing others a favor when we forgive them. But we are mostly helping ourselves, because when we hate someone or hold bitter feelings and grudges toward them, we are really hurting ourselves more than them. Refusing to forgive, even when the other person is neither sorry nor repentant, fills our souls with spiritual poison. It keeps past wounds from healing and prevents us from moving forward toward the Lord. And if we don't cleanse that spiritual poison with an act of total forgiveness and forgetting, it will rot and fester inside us until we are miserable and we probably won't even understand why.

> When our grievance grows to hatred, we become slaves of the very persons we hate. We are bound to them with chains that leave us no peace. Waking, we are haunted by their presence. Our sleeping is shadowed by their deeds. Our memories are clouded by their wrongdoing. Their present actions grind and gore us. We have allowed hatred to become our incarceration. (Karen Burton Mains, *The Key To A Loving Heart*, Carmel, New York, Guidepost Books, 1979, p. 78.)

H. Burke Peterson warned, "The longer the poison of resentment and unforgiveness stays in a body, the greater and longer lasting is its destructive effect. As long as we blame others for our condition or circumstance and build a wall of self-justification around ourselves, our strength will diminish and our power and ability to rise above our situation will fade away. The poison of revenge, or of unforgiving thoughts or attitudes, unless removed, will destroy the soul in which it is harbored." (*Ensign*, November 1983, p. 59.) On the other hand, the more forgiving we are toward those who hurt us, the more we will receive and feel the Father's forgiveness for our own mistakes. How could we possibly expect to draw close to the Savior when we reject the power of his atonement by clinging to our resentments toward others?

What if I Cannot Forgive?

Sooner or later, every person will suffer a personal injury or injustice so painful that it will seem impossible to feel forgiving. Letting go of the pain will be beyond our mortal ability because the wounds are so deep. But the Lord has provided a way out of this problem.

Contrary to what we might think, forgiving does not always start with our emotions. We cannot always turn our emotions off like a faucet, and the Lord doesn't expect us to. Forgiveness begins with a decision—a mental decision. No matter how deep the wound, we can always decide to be willing to forgive, and that is the starting point. The Savior stated that he "requireth the heart and a willing mind." (D&C 64:34.) Paul explained this starting point when he said, "If there be first a willing mind, (then) it is accepted according to that (which) a man hath, and not according to that (which) he hath not." (2 Corinthians 8:12.) In other words, if we are willing to forgive, if we are willing to let go; willing to bear the injustice without complaining about it, God will reward that willingness with a deep sense of peace and comfort, even love for the one who offended us. We will not be condemned because we are unable to forgive without divine assistance.

In his role as our Savior, only Jesus Christ can save us from the emotions we cannot overcome by ourselves. This he *can* do and this he is *eager* to do. If we will make the decision to be willing to forgive, the Savior will honor that choice by coming into our lives and removing from us all the painful emotions which have chained us to the burdens of the past. So forgiving isn't dependent upon a tough will power or a thick skin. It is based upon faith in Christ and his merciful atonement. Forgiving others is probably one of the hardest things Christ has asked us to do, but he doesn't expect us to do it by ourselves.

But what can we do when our pain is so great that we are not even *willing* to forgive? What about the situations where we are consumed with anger and a desire for revenge? Even then there is hope if we will humble ourselves by laying that anger and hate on the altar of sacrifice, as we offer a prayer of surrender. We might pray in this manner: "Father, there is no way I can forgive this by myself. In fact, to be honest, I don't even *want* to forgive this person. But I know that attitude is wrong. I know refusing to forgive is harmful, both to the other persons involved and to myself. So Heavenly Father, I am asking thee to help me surrender my bitterness. I am asking thee to make me willing to be willing."

We know that he will respond to such a prayer because Christ himself gave the assurance, "I say unto you, all among them who know their hearts are honest, and are broken, and their spirits contrite, and are willing to observe their covenants by sacrifice—yea, every sacrifice which I, the Lord, shall command—they are accepted of me." (D&C 97:8.)

Yes, we can actually pray for divine assistance to make us willing to be willing. Sherrie Johnson said, "Only by forgiving and forgetting, letting go of our bitterness and hurt, do we free ourselves to progress. Change of any kind is difficult, but forgiving and forgetting is perhaps the hardest kind of change. This change is beyond yourself, but is attainable when you seek and accept the help of Heavenly Father. He can give you the strength you lack." (*Ensign,* January 1985, p. 60.)

The miracle that takes place as the Savior of mankind saves us from our pain and removes the harmful emotions which have held us captive is amazing. One sister related how the Savior released her from the deep resentment she felt toward a relative who had abused her as a child, leaving her with a permanent, painful physical condition. She often wondered at the injustice of the suffering the abuse had caused and why she had to continue suffering, even as an adult. One day, as she listened to a talk in church, her heart was touched. The Spirit bore witness to her that she should forgive the man who had wronged her and that she could do so with the help of the Lord Jesus Christ. When she finally surrendered this terrible injustice to the Savior, she was set free. She said:

The price for that sin has already been paid by him in Gethsemane. I have no right to hold on to it and demand justice, so I gladly hand it back to him and rejoice in his love and mercy. My heart is so full of joy, peace, and gratitude and love! Words cannot express my feelings. (Personal correspondence.)

Every person on this planet is capable of weakness and sin. Those who have injured us are vulnerable, imperfect human beings just as we are. God does not demand perfection of us and we have no right to demand perfection of those who hurt us. Remembering this will help us to separate the offense from the offender. It is also helpful to view those who repeatedly hurt us as being handicapped. Wouldn't it be easier to forgive them for hurting us if they were physically crippled or blind? Perhaps they are blind emotionally. Perhaps they can't see how they hurt others. Perhaps, because of unfortunate circumstances in their past, they just don't know any other way of relating to you. For all we know, their unacceptable behavior may be nothing more than a reflection of the way they were injured in their youth. If we could see into their hearts as God can, we would understand their deviant behavior and not condemn them for it.

When we get right down to it, aren't we *all* handicapped in one way or another? Aren't we all in need of the Lord's grace to compensate for our imperfections? Christ has promised to take such disadvantages into account when he judges us, actually "suiting his mercies according to the conditions of the children of men." (D&C 46:15.) Since God is so willing to make allowances for our imperfections, shouldn't we follow his example?

We are sure to encounter many injuries which we will not be capable of forgiving by ourselves. Satan will seize upon such wounds to separate us from the love of Christ, but we must not allow him to do so. No matter how great our pain, we can always choose to forgive, or at least choose to be willing to be willing. And when we offer that sacrifice of obedience to his command to "forgive all men," Christ will not only heal our wounds and do the work within us which we were incapable of doing without his help, but he will also reward us with peace and comfort and the joy of his fellowship.

Forgiving ourselves and others freely will always lead us to a closer relationship with the magnificent Savior who makes mercy and forgiveness possible.

Growing Closer Through Adversity

When we accepted Heavenly Father's plan for a mortal probation we each agreed to his condition that we must experience "an opposition in all things." (2 Nephi 2:11.) Some opposition comes through the unwanted circumstances we know as adversities, trials, tribulations and suffering. It makes little difference whether a particular situation was deliberately caused by God, or merely occurred in consequence of the imperfections of this mortal world. If we allow it, God will use these circumstances to test, tutor and develop the divine nature within us. Therefore, one of the keys to drawing closer to the Savior and Heavenly Father is to have a positive, patient attitude about the problems that come into our lives. This is not always easy. Let me share a page from my journal:

Today was a disaster. It began when my wife and daughter called from across town, because our tired old station wagon wouldn't start and they were stranded. I drove over in our Volkswagen bus, taking the three children we were babysitting that day. I finally got the car going by adjusting the points, only to have to turn it off because of the racket the engine was making. To my embarrassment, I discovered it was two quarts low on oil.

After finding a gas station to buy the two quarts of oil, the battery was dead and the darn car wouldn't even start with jumper cables. We had to leave it there until I could come back with a new battery.

Later that day our oldest daughter, Jeri Ann, got a ticket for driving through a red light which she couldn't see because her diabetes was out of balance. Later that afternoon they called us from Jeri's work because she had lapsed into a diabetic coma. We rushed to her work and took her to the emergency room at the hospital. They put her into intensive care.

While at the hospital, someone smashed into the back of our car, crumpling the left rear end. They did not even leave a note to say how we could contact them.

To top off the day, that evening I caught Kristy, our 18 month old daughter, drinking the dog's water. Ugh!

Sometimes in the midst of such troubles, it is hard to believe that any good can come from them. Looking back at this day, I can see we learned from it, and some of it seems pretty funny now, but it sure didn't feel that way then. Paul taught, "No chastening for the present seemeth to be joyous, but grievous: nevertheless afterward it yieldeth the peaceable fruit of righteousness unto them which are exercised thereby." (Hebrews 12:11.) We cannot always choose the obstacles we face, but we can always decide whether we will allow them to discourage and pull us down or lead us to a closer dependence upon our Savior. The Savior promised that "all things wherewith you have been afflicted shall work together for your good, and to my name's glory." (D&C 98:3.) Thus it was that Lehi could promise his son that in spite of the fact that "thou hast suffered afflictions and much sorrow . . . thou knowest the greatness of God; and he shall consecrate thine afflictions for thy gain." (2 Nephi 2:1-2.)

Steven, (insert your name) "Search diligently, pray always, and be believing, and [Steven,] all things shall work together for your good, if ye walk

uprightly and remember the covenant wherewith ye
have covenanted one with another. (D&C 90:24.)

There are many circumstances which seem so hopeless
and devastating that it truly takes "diligent searching" to
find God's purpose in them. Someday, on the other side of
eternity, we will be able to look back over life's adversities
and see divine purpose in them as they gave us experience,
built character, and helped us learn how much we needed
the Savior in our daily lives. The Savior explained, "My people must be tried in all things, that they may be prepared
to receive the glory that I have for them." (D&C 136:31.)
You can test this principle of divine purpose in adversity by
tracing the pattern of your own experience. Examine a situation in your life which now brings you great joy. Trace it
back through the genealogy of circumstance that preceded
the present victory, and you will inevitably find that its
roots lie in some challenge of the past, some weakness or
difficulty which once gave you great sorrow.

The Savior offered encouragement to bear with our sorrows when he said "He that is faithful in tribulation, the
reward of the same is greater in the kingdom of heaven."
(D&C 58:2.) What a small price to pay for fellowship with
the one who suffered the most of all. If we would be close
to the Lord, we must be "willing to submit to all things
which the Lord seeth fit to inflict upon [us], even as a
child doth submit to his father." (Mosiah 3:19.)

My wife has a deep, enduring trust and faith in the
Lord's compassion, but one day, while deeply troubled by
her adversities, she cried out to the Lord in prayer,
"Sometimes you make it awfully hard for me to believe in
you." Even before the echo of her accusation had died
away, she felt his reply in the kindest voice, "My daughter,
sometimes you make it hard for me to believe in you."

We must not make the mistake of assuming
that problems are evidence of the Lord's inatten-
tion. On the contrary, many of life's most
discouraging situations can [develop] our strengths
and weaknesses in ways unmatched by prosperity
and success, enabling us to focus our energy on

developing a Christlike character. (Larry W. Tippetts, *Ensign*, June 1989, p. 57.)

A little blind girl was sitting on her father's lap on the front porch when a long-time friend of the family came into the yard. Quietly climbing the front steps, he winked at his friend as he grabbed the daughter from her father's arms, and ran down the steps and up the sidewalk. Soon he stopped, amazed because the girl had made no effort to struggle or cry out. "Why aren't you frightened?" he asked. "You didn't know who had you in his arms, did you?"

"I didn't have to know," she answered. "My daddy knew, and that was good enough for me." (See Don Baker, *Acceptance*, Portland Oregon: Multnomah Press, 1985, p. 89.)

We are often blind to the divine purpose behind our difficult and unwanted experiences. Can we, like this little girl, be content in the knowledge that God knows what is happening and that he is always in control, working to bring good out of what appears to be a disadvantage? Or must we, in our faithlessness, shout and scream for an accounting of why this is happening to us?

The Bible counsels us to "Trust in the Lord with all thine heart; and lean not unto thine own understanding. In all thy ways acknowledge him, and he shall direct thy paths." (Proverbs 3:5-6.) What better reason could we possibly have for trusting the Lord in the midst of our adversities than the promise of his personal guidance? If we are not willing to trust him in the midst of our difficulties, then how can we claim to trust him in anything? When we fully trust the Lord, we do not worry about all the unpleasant consequences of our adversity. Rather, we simply struggle forward doing the best we can, knowing that he is a God of power and that his divine purposes will be fulfilled on our behalf.

In those times of great adversity when it is all we can do to hang on and wait for relief, it is not *what* we know about the gospel that will sustain us, but *who* we know. If we know Jesus Christ, our personal Shepherd, then all else will fall into place. Building a relationship with him during the good times makes it easier to feel and know his sustaining presence during the tough times.

Becoming a "new creature in Christ" is not easy, nor is it instantaneous. Receiving the "new birth" or the "mighty change" in our hearts and sinful natures is not an *event*, but rather a *process* of growth. Just as mortal birth requires months of preparation and is delivered through the suffering of great pain, so it is with the spiritual rebirth. If we would receive the new heart and nature that Christ is working to give us, then we must be willing to bear the pains of adversity with trust and patience, without resentment, complaint, or doubt. Job set the standard when he said, "Though he slay me, yet will I trust in him." (Job 13:15.)

Paul said, "We must through much tribulation enter into the kingdom of God." (Acts 14:22.) When we come before Christ in the day of judgment, it will not be trophies, medals or great achievements that he will be looking for. He will be far more interested in our response to the difficulties we encountered. He that bears the scars of crucifixion will be looking to see what scars we bear from our own adversities. And our hearts will tell him what those trials have led us to become.

The Savior commanded us to "Be patient in tribulation until I come." (D&C 54:10.) This edict is not easy to obey, because we are often more anxious for the trouble to pass than we are to learn the lesson the adversity is meant to teach us. The Savior also said, "As many as I love, I rebuke and chasten: be zealous therefore, and repent." And, "My people must needs be chastened until they learn obedience, if it must needs be, by the things which they suffer." (D&C 105:6.) Suffering may sound like a tough way to learn, but even "though [Christ] were a son, yet learned he obedience by the things which he suffered." (Hebrews 5:8.) Why should we expect to have it easier than the Savior?

Actually, it is our own stubbornness that determines how difficult our lessons have to be. Jesus Christ loves us enough to do whatever it takes, no matter how tough it gets, to win our loyalty and devotion and to cleanse our lives of the things that keep us from his fellowship. Brigham Young taught that "Every trial and experience you have passed through is necessary for your salvation." (*Discourses of Brigham Young*, Salt Lake City: Deseret Book,

1954, p. 345.) If we resist the lessons he provides, if we rebel and refuse to learn, the afflictions will be repeated over and over, with greater and greater intensity, until we finally humble ourselves and learn what we need to change.

As we seek to draw closer to the Savior, he welcomes our approach by revealing to us the imperfections which are preventing the fellowship we seek. Keeping this in mind, we should rejoice in the insight his reproof provides, and "despise not the chastening of the Lord; neither be weary of his correction." (Proverbs 3:11.) Every chastening or affliction that comes into our life, whether by divine intent or mere circumstance, opens the door to a closer relationship with the Savior and Heavenly Father.

> And ye have forgotten the exhortation which speaketh unto you as unto children, My son, despise not thou the chastening of the Lord, nor faint when thou art rebuked of him:
> For whom the Lord loveth he chasteneth, and scourgeth every son whom he receiveth. (Hebrews 12:5-6.)

Christ has encouraged us to hang on with patience, when our trials seem to chafe and have no purpose. Steven, (insert your name) "If thou wilt do good, yea, and hold out faithful to the end, thou shalt be saved in the kingdom of God." (D&C 6:13.) Sometimes all we can do is grit our teeth and hang on. Most of the time we will not be able to manipulate our circumstances to our liking. But if we are willing to hang on and remain faithful, Christ has promised to honor that persistence by providing strength and being with us throughout the difficulty. It is amazing how much we can bear when we know the Savior is going through it with us. Ardeth G. Kapp said, "There will be some steep climbs ahead, but our Lord and Savior, Jesus Christ, has covenanted and promised to climb with each of us every step of the way." (*Ensign*, November 1986, p. 89.) But we will not *know* that he is with us if we allow ourselves to be filled with bitterness, anger and resentment.

While patience in adversity is often thought of as a passive trait, it actually requires great faith and trust in the Savior's watchful care. Neal A. Maxwell defined patience as "a willingness, in a sense, to watch the unfolding purposes of God with a sense of wonder and awe—rather than pacing up and down within the cell of our circumstance." (*Ensign*, October 1980, pp. 28-29.) The principle to keep in mind when we feel impatient with our adversity is that God has promised to "order all things for [our] good, as fast as [we] are able to receive them." (D&C 111:11.) How foolish and arrogant it is to stamp our feet and throw a spiritual tantrum when his perfect will dictates a slower process of growth than we want or when circumstances seem totally unfair to us. Patience in adversity demonstrates trust in Christ's divine providence. Impatience, anxiety and resentment deny that confidence and prevents the fellowship we are seeking.

The Lord never said that every situation here would be fair. But he does guarantee that the compensating rewards will come, if not in this life then in the next, and that makes it worth any price we have to pay. As we seek to grow closer to Christ and Heavenly Father, let's cling to the knowledge that all things will be made right in the Lord's good time, and that no matter how tough our difficulties seem now, they will be but a moment in the eternal view of things.

Alma promised that "whosoever shall put their trust in God shall be supported in their trials, and their troubles, and their afflictions." (Alma 36:3.) Elder Ronald E. Poelman said that it is by receiving that divine support through these spiritual refinements that "we may be prepared to experience personal and direct contact with God." (*Ensign*, May 1989, p. 24.) Thus, the very circumstances which could have pulled us away from the Lord can now bring us into a closer relationship with our Friend and Shepherd. Because our trusting, submissive attitude in spite of adversity allows Christ to draw closer to us, we will come to treasure that adversity as one of our most valued experiences.

Growing Closer Through Gratitude

And he who receiveth all things with thankfulness shall be made glorious. (D&C 78:19.)

Why does the attitude of gratitude lead us to glory? Because it draws us closer to Christ. We cannot be close to the Savior, nor can we fellowship with Heavenly Father, until we learn to appreciate what they have done for us. There is a spiritual formula here: the more grateful we are, the closer God will be; the less grateful we are, the farther away he will seem.

Gratitude opens the door to divine fellowship.

There are three words which cannot be separated from the attitude of gratitude. They are prayer, praise and worship. Through prayer we *express* our gratitude. Through praise and worship we *demonstrate* our gratitude. If we are truly thankful for our blessings, words of praise and worship will naturally flow from our hearts continually. Indeed, a constant, unceasing attitude of gratitude is one of the most frequent commandments in the scriptures. "Nevertheless thy vows [and expressions of gratitude] shall be offered up in righteousness on all days and at all times." (D&C 59:11.) "Worship God, in whatsoever place ye may be in . . . and . . . live in thanksgiving daily, for the many mercies and blessings which he doth bestow upon you." (Alma 34:38.)

We are commanded to offer our praise and thanksgiving in both the morning and evening as we arise and retire. We are to arise "every morning to thank and praise the Lord, and likewise at even." (1 Chronicles 23:30.) We are to "pray unto him continually by day, and give thanks unto his holy name by night." (2 Nephi 9:52.)

Steven, (insert your name) "Counsel with the Lord in all thy doings, and he will direct thee for good; yea, [and Steven,] when thou liest down at night lie down unto the Lord, that he may watch over you in your sleep; and when thou risest in the morning let thy heart be full of thanks unto God; and [Steven,] if ye do these things, ye shall be lifted up at the last day. (Alma 37:37.)

Our expressions of gratitude should include more than mere thanks for blessings received. When our thanksgiving extends into expressions of appreciation for the attributes of God's perfect goodness, we open the door to closer fellowship with him. Each time we pray we should ponder the Lord's attributes and then "give thanks at the remembrance of his holiness." (Psalms 97:12.) "Oh that men would praise the Lord of his goodness, and for his wonderful works to the children of men!" (Psalms 107:8.) As the magnificence of God's perfect love and concern for us distills upon our hearts, we will "Praise him for his mighty acts," and we will almost involuntarily, spontaneously "praise him according to his excellent greatness." (Psalms 150:2.)

Praise ye the Lord. O give thanks unto the Lord; for he is good: for his mercy endureth for ever. (Psalms 106:1.)

I will bless the Lord at all times: his praise shall continually be in my mouth. (Psalms 34:1.)

President Marion G. Romney said that "we should be thankful and express appreciation for all favors we receive, and surely we receive many. The chief objects of our gratitude, however, should be, and are, God, our Heavenly Father, and his Son Jesus Christ, our Lord and Redeemer." (*Ensign,* June 1974, p. 3.)

As we express gratitude to the Lord for his divine attributes we are worshiping who he is as well as what he is. Therefore, "I will praise the name of God . . . and will magnify him with thanksgiving." (Psalms 69:30.)

Give unto the Lord the glory due unto his name; worship the Lord in the beauty of holiness. (Psalms 29:2.)

One way that we worship the Lord and attribute to him the "glory due his name" is to ask his help in overcoming our difficulties. Asking for his help is a form of worship. It is an acknowledgement that all good things come from his kindness and love. "And, behold, there came a leper and worshipped him, saying, Lord, if thou wilt, thou canst make me clean." (Matthew 8:2.) And "there came a certain ruler, and worshipped him, saying, My daughter is even now dead: but come and lay thy hand upon her, and she shall live." (Matthew 9:18.) And further, "Then came she and worshipped him, saying, Lord, help me." (Matthew 15:25.)

Thus we see that we must "in every thing by prayer and supplication with thanksgiving let [our] requests be made known unto God." (Philippians 4:6.) President Marion G. Romney said, "To thank the Lord in all things is not merely a courtesy, it is a commandment as binding upon us as any other commandment." (*Ensign*, November 1982, p. 50.)

Thou shalt thank the Lord thy God in all things," and "in every thing give thanks: for this is the will of God in Christ Jesus concerning you. (D&C 59:7; 1 Thessalonians 5:18.)

It is easy to give thanks when we are receiving blessings and avoiding difficulties. Thus, "If thou art merry, praise the Lord . . . with a prayer of praise and thanksgiving." (D&C 136:28.) Indeed, "Ye must give thanks unto God in the Spirit for whatsoever blessings ye are blessed with," always "returning thanks unto God for whatsoever things ye do receive." (D&C 46:32; Alma 7:23.)

But true gratitude is shown when we are able to trust, appreciate and express thankfulness to the Lord in spite of difficult and unwanted circumstances. Nephi, for example, while in pain from his bonds and even while under the threat of death, said, "Nevertheless, I did look unto my God, and I did praise him all the day long; and I did not murmur against the Lord because of mine afflictions." (1 Nephi 18:16.) Similarly, while Paul and Silas were imprisoned for preaching Christ, they nevertheless "prayed, and sang praises unto God." (Acts 16:25.) It is this kind of gratitude in spite of difficult circumstances that prompted the Psalmist to say, "I will offer to thee the sacrifice of thanksgiving, and will call upon the name of the Lord." (Psalms 116:17.)

Sometimes it does require sacrifice to express gratitude for situations that hurt and cause unwanted difficulties, but great blessings follow such worship. We may have to pray something like: "Father, I don't understand this affliction. I don't like it and I wish it hadn't happened. But Father, I believe thy promise that all things can work together for my good, and I'm claiming that promise now because I surely can't see any good in it yet. I thank thee for thine intervention on my behalf and ask thee to show me the purpose of this difficulty that I may be even more grateful."

Heavenly Father is not offended by such a prayer. He delights to prove his power on our behalf when we are trusting and grateful even before his divine providence is manifest. On the other hand, the Lord has said that it does offend and anger him when we fail to recognize and confess his influence in our day-to-day lives. (See D&C 59:21.) President Joseph F. Smith said, "I believe that one of the greatest sins of which the inhabitants of the earth are guilty today is the sin of ingratitude, the want of acknowledgement, on their part, of God and his right to govern and control. Because of this, God is not pleased with the inhabitants of the earth but is angry with them because they will not acknowledge his hand in all things." (*Gospel Doctrine*, 5th Ed., Salt Lake City Utah: Deseret Book, 1939, pp. 270-271; emphasis added.)

Let me illustrate how changing our feelings of resentment and frustration into feelings of gratitude can bring us closer to the Lord. Many years ago, I received permission to perform a personal service project of "skinning" the tall palm trees at our Stake building. I had never done this before and was quite apprehensive about the project because it required me to climb high to the top of each tree with no support but a chain around me and the trunk of the tree and steel spikes strapped to my ankles, inasmuch as the trees were too tall for ladders.

Over a period of several months I spent about sixty hours hanging there on the pivot points of those tiny spikes while trimming the trees. There was a constant flow of dust, bugs and spider webs as I trimmed the branches away. The straps that held the spikes to my ankles made deep indentations and bruises in my legs. My ankles hurt with excruciating pain each time I had to move around the tree and drive the spikes into a new spot. The pain was so great that I could never work more than a couple of hours and then it required several days to recuperate before I could go back. This constant pain, plus the fright and insecurity I felt from hanging so precariously from the tops of the tall trees made it a very difficult project.

On one particularly painful day, I hung there on a tree and wept in self-pity and regret at having volunteered for such an unpleasant task. As I wished that I could find an excuse to abandon the project, the Spirit gently whispered a reminder that Jesus had also hung in pain; pain for me. He had no safety belt to hold him up, but hung from the cross with the nails tearing at his flesh. Instead of coming down to safety and recuperation after a couple of hours, his pain continued until it resulted in death. And his death was to set me free. Instead of merely being inconvenienced by dust and dirt in his face, he hung there in agony from the burden of my sins. And yet, the Spirit whispered, "Although in agony he hung, no murmuring word escaped his tongue."

With shame at my ingratitude, I continued my work. My legs still hurt, but there was a new determination within me to bear any pain, to make any sacrifice within my power to show my devotion and gratitude to him who so willingly demonstrated his love for me.

It is a good thing to give thanks unto the Lord, and to sing praises unto thy name, O most High. (Psalms 92:1.)

Face to Face

Our final assignment in growing closer to the Savior is to accept his invitation to grow in spirituality, commitment and devotion until we gain the power to part the veil and behold him face to face. Christ has emphasized that this "is your privilege, and a promise I give unto you . . . that inasmuch as you strip yourselves from jealousies and fears, and humble yourselves before me, for ye are not sufficiently humble, the veil shall be rent and you shall see me and know that I am." (D&C 67:10.) We notice that the Savior did not say this promise could be fulfilled, or might be fulfilled. What he did promise is that when we are sufficiently prepared, the veil shall be rent.

Here is another version of the same invitation and promise: "Verily, thus saith the Lord: It shall come to pass that every soul who forsaketh his sins and cometh unto me, and calleth on my name, and obeyeth my voice, and keepeth my commandments, shall see my face and know that I am." (D&C 93:1.) Speaking of this verse, President Joseph Fielding Smith said, "This promise is unto all men everywhere so that all may know if they will." (*Improvement Era*, Vol. 33, p. 726, as cited in *Ensign*, August 1975, p. 21.) And Elder Jacob de Jager of the First Quorum of Seventy said of the same verse, "Every person who is sufficiently faithful and sufficiently spiritual has the promise that God himself will appear to him." (*Devotional Speeches of the Year, Provo*, Utah: Brigham

Young University Press, 1988-89, p. 89.) Speaking of the same promise, the prophet Joseph Smith said:

> After any portion of the human family are made acquainted with the important fact that there is a God, who has created and does uphold all things, the extent of their knowledge respecting his character and glory will depend upon their diligence and faithfulness in seeking after him, until, like Enoch, the brother of Jared, and Moses, they shall obtain faith in God, and power with him to behold him face to face. (*Lectures on Faith*, no. 2, N.B. Lundwall, compiler and publisher, p. 23.)

The Savior is working continually to penetrate our mortal preoccupations so that we can be closer to him. "He that hath my commandments, and keepeth them, he it is that loveth me: and he that loveth me shall be loved of my Father, and I will love him, and will manifest myself to him." (John 14:21.) We could personalize this verse to read: Steven, (insert your name) "If you keep my commandments it will show that you love me, and you will be loved of my Father, and [Steven], I will love you and manifest myself to you." After making this astounding announcement, the Savior immediately repeated the promise, stating, "If a man love me, he will keep my words: and my Father will love him, and we will come unto him, and make our abode with him." (John 14:23.) Or personalized: Steven, "if you love me you will keep my words. And my Father will love you, and we will come unto you, and [Steven,] we will make our abode with you." Many who have not experienced a personal visitation from the Savior have tried to interpret these two verses as symbolic, rather than admitting they mean exactly what they say. However, speaking of verse 23, Joseph Smith was inspired to record: "The appearing of the Father and Son, in that verse, is a personal appearance." (D&C 130:3.)

The Holy Ghost was described by Christ as "The Comforter." (See John 14:16-17, 26.) But in addition to the ministry of that Comforter, Jesus promised the ministry of a second comforter, referring to his personal appearance to the faithful. "I will not leave you comfortless," he said, but "I [myself] will come to you." (John 14:18.) Of this promise, the Prophet Joseph Smith explained:

> Now what is this other Comforter? It is not more nor less than the Lord Jesus Christ Himself; and this is the sum and substance of the whole matter; that when any man obtains this last Comforter, he will have the personage of Jesus Christ to attend him, or appear unto him, from time to time, and even He will manifest the Father unto him, and they will take up their abode with him, and the visions of the heavens will be opened unto him, and the Lord will teach him face to face. (*Teachings Of The Prophet Joseph Smith*, 7th Edition, Comp. Joseph Fielding Smith, Salt Lake City, Utah: Deseret Book, 1951, pp. 150-151.)

It is the opportunity of all those who have received the authorized ordinances under the authority of the Melchizedek Priesthood "to have the privilege of receiving the mysteries of the kingdom of heaven, to have the heavens opened unto them . . . and to enjoy the communion and presence of God the Father, and Jesus the mediator of the new covenant." (D&C 107:19.) This privilege has been offered to God's children for thousands of years.

> Now this Moses plainly taught to the children of Israel in the wilderness, and sought diligently to sanctify his people that they might behold the face of God; But they hardened their hearts and could not endure his presence. (D&C 84:23-24.)

Because the children of Israel refused to lift themselves spiritually to receive this great privilege, "the Lord in his wrath, for his anger was kindled against them, swore that they should not enter into his rest while in the wilderness, which rest is the fullness of his glory. Therefore, he took Moses out of their midst, and the Holy Priesthood also." (D&C 84:24-25.)

The children of Israel were unable to measure up to this "privilege and promise" because they refused to prepare themselves spiritually, "for [God and Christ] are only to be seen and understood by the power of the Holy Spirit, which God bestows on those who love him, and purify themselves before him; To whom he grants this privilege of seeing and knowing for themselves; That through the power and manifestation of the Spirit, while in the flesh, they may be able to bear his presence in the world of glory." (D&C 76:116-118.)

This "privilege and promise" is more than an interesting invitation. Working to part the veil and meet our Savior face to face is actually a commandment. Jesus said, Steven, (insert your name) "Seek the face of the Lord always." (D&C 101:38.) Other scriptures repeat the command: "Seek his face continually," and "Seek his face evermore." (1 Chronicles 16:11; Psalms 105:4.) "Seek" is a verb. Seeking the Lord's face should be the goal of every disciple. "To worship the Lord," said Bruce R. McConkie, "is to follow after him, to seek his face, to believe his doctrine, and to think his thoughts." (*Ensign*, December 1971, p. 130.)

We begin our quest by cultivating a strong desire to see him and then expressing that desire by praying to see his face. Satan would have us believe such a prayer is presumptuous and he would try to distract our effort by accusing us of seeking for signs or miracles. But it is not presumptuous to pray for the privilege of piercing the veil if we do it in humble obedience to the Lord's command and invitation, for he himself has instructed, "Seek ye the Lord while he may be found, call ye upon him while he is near." (Isaiah 55:6.) Our response to this commandment should be, "When thou saidst, Seek ye my face; my heart said unto thee, Thy face, Lord, will I seek." (Psalms 27:8.)

Let us not be satisfied with mere activity in church. Let's not wait for the next life to find our status with God, because we can do it now. Seek to become a friend to the Savior. Tell the Lord in humble but persistent prayer that you want to know him as he has invited and commanded.

The strength of our desire to see the Lord face to face, and our faith in this principle will grow in proportion to the purity of our mind and heart. Christ validated the privilege of seeing God face to face when he said, "Blessed are the pure in heart: for they *shall* see God." (Matthew 5:8; emphasis added.) No person with unclean or impure thoughts will have power to pierce the veil before the day of judgment.

> Therefore, sanctify yourselves that your minds become single to God, and the days will come that you shall see him, for he will unveil his face unto you. (D&C 88:68.)

The Savior does not expect us to achieve this level of purity instantly, on a whim, or by wishful thinking. "Ye must practice virtue and holiness before me continually," he counseled, (D&C 46:33.) Spiritual maturity, purity and sanctification take time. But as we improve, our confidence will grow in direct proportion to our progress. "Let virtue garnish thy thoughts unceasingly," the Savior challenged and promised that as we do learn to do so, "then shall thy confidence wax strong in the presence of God; and . . . the Holy Ghost shall be thy constant companion." (D&C 121:45-46.) Why is it essential to attain the constant companionship of the Holy Ghost when it is Christ we are trying to meet? Because "he manifesteth himself unto all those who believe in him, by the power of the holy Ghost . . . according to their faith." (2 Nephi 26:13.)

Amazingly, it is largely up to us when this blessing occurs in our life. The scriptures teach that we can actually attain a level of faith where Christ cannot keep from coming to us! We are familiar with the premortal Christ's appearance to the brother of Jared. Many, however, do not realize that his piercing of the veil was because of his great faith, not because the Savior had planned to show himself. There were many others who achieved similar visitations because of their faith.

> And there were many whose faith was so exceeding strong, even before Christ came, who could not be kept from within the veil, but truly saw with their eyes the things which they had beheld with an eye of faith, and they were glad.

And behold, we have seen in this record that one of these was the brother of Jared; for so great was his faith in God, that when God put forth his finger he could not hide it from the sight of the brother of Jared . . . .

And after the brother of Jared had beheld the finger of the Lord, because of the promise which [he] had obtained by faith, the Lord could not withhold anything from his sight; wherefore he showed him all things, for he could no longer be kept without the veil." (Ether 12:19-21; see also Ether 3:1-20.)

This scripture is included in the Book of Mormon to testify and teach of what we too may experience. For "in that day that they shall exercise faith in me, saith the Lord, even as the brother of Jared did, that they may become sanctified in me, then will I manifest unto them the things which the brother of Jared saw, even to the unfolding unto them all my revelations, saith Jesus Christ, the Son of God." (Ether 4:7.) President Joseph Fielding Smith has said of our power to pierce the veil once we are qualified:

If we would put into practice the great doctrines which have been revealed in the revelations contained in the holy scriptures, it would only be a matter of a very short time until this great people would be in the same condition, absolutely, as were the people in the city of Enoch.

We would be able to walk with God, we would be able to behold his face, because then faith would abound in the hearts of the people to the extent that it would be impossible for the Lord to withhold himself, and he would reveal himself unto us as he has done in times past. (*Doctrines of Salvation*, Salt Lake City, Utah: Bookcraft, Inc., 1954, Vol 1, pp. 3-4.)

While it is possible for us to reach for this blessing according to our desires, and while faith can have the power to pierce the veil, the Lord will certainly not allow this to happen before we are ready to bear the responsibility which accompanies such manifestations. Therefore, he has stressed, "he will unveil his face unto you, [but] it shall be in his own time, and in his own way, and according to his own will." (D&C 88:68.)

As we patiently, trustingly wait upon the Lord's timing, we continue to do all we can to prepare ourselves by working toward the constant companionship of the Holy Ghost, purifying our lives and building the Kingdom of God. We must not allow feelings of discouragement to enter our hearts if Christ does not appear as soon as we had hoped. The path may be long. It most certainly will be filled with obstacles and tests to prepare us for this magnificent experience. To those not yet prepared to receive the Lord, he has commanded patience and perseverance in our quest: "Behold, ye are little children and ye cannot bear all things now; ye must grow in grace and in the knowledge of the truth." (D&C 50:40.) "Continue in patience until ye are perfected," he further encouraged, and "let not your minds turn back; and when ye are worthy, in mine own due time, ye shall see and know that which was conferred upon you by the hands of my servant Joseph Smith, Jun." (D&C 67:13-14.)

Each insight we receive and then honor will lead us to a higher level of spirituality, and then another and another until Christ has become our very best friend, and stepping through the veil to meet him face to face will be a natural culmination of years of preparation. Until that time, as we reach toward the promise, learning line upon line to be closer and closer, we can each work on first parting the veil enough to reach through and feel the Lord's presence and know he is there for us. We must each pass through the mists of darkness as we move toward the tree of life, which symbolizes the Savior's love. But as Bruce C. Hafen has so eloquently expressed, as we cling to the iron rod, "we are likely to find that the cold rod of iron will begin to feel in our hands as the warm, firm, loving hand of one who is literally pulling us along the way." And as we learn to cling to the Savior, as we learn to feel his presence more strongly each day, "he gives us strength enough to rescue us, warmth enough to tell us that home is not far away; and we summon our deepest resources to reciprocate with our own renewed energy until we are again 'at one' in the arms of the Lord through the power of his great 'at-one-ment.' ." (*The Broken Heart*, Salt Lake City, Utah: Deseret Book, 1989, p. 22.)

In the 46th section of the Doctrine and Covenants we are given a detailed description of the gifts of the Spirit, two of which pertain to knowing and seeing the Savior face to face. In verse thirteen the first and most desirable gift is described: "To some it is given by the Holy Ghost to know that Jesus Christ is the Son of God, and that he was crucified for the sins of the world." (D&C 46:13.)

We all know people who have been blessed with a powerful testimony of the divinity, power and atonement of Jesus Christ. But not everyone is granted this deep, personal insight to begin with. For some, perhaps even for most of us, in the beginning of our quest there is a second, more easily attained gift that provides a starting point that each person can use to begin their relationship. "To others it is given to believe on their words." (D&C 46:14.) That is to say, there is a gift of the Spirit which enables us to know the Savior vicariously by believing on the words of those who are given the direct witness of the Spirit described in verse thirteen. This may seem disappointing and insufficient. It is not. It is sufficient to attain eternal life. Let us read the entire verse: "To others it is given to believe on their words, that they also might have eternal life if they continue faithful." (D&C 46:14.)

> It is true that the scriptures speak of a companionship with the Father and the Son that is granted to those who have become wholly pure . . . but one of the things I have come to know for myself . . . is that the Lord offers us an earlier companionship while we are yet impure. That earlier relationship is, in fact, the only thing that can make us pure." (Colin B. Douglas, *Ensign*, April 1989, pp. 14-15.)

Two years before Melvin J. Ballard was called as an apostle, he met the Savior face to face in a dream in which he was taken into the Salt Lake temple. He said, "I was led into a room where I was informed I was to meet someone.

As I entered the room I saw, seated on a raised platform, the most glorious being I have ever conceived of, and was taken forward to be introduced to Him. As I approached He smiled, called my name, and stretched out His hands toward me. If I live to be a million years old I shall never forget that smile. He put his arms around me and kissed me, as He took me into His bosom, and He blessed me until my whole being was thrilled."

While many have described this privilege of meeting their Savior, perhaps no one has better described the feeling this sacred experience invokes then Elder Ballard. He continued, "As He finished I fell at His feet, and there saw the marks of the nails; and as I kissed them, with deep joy swelling through my whole being, I felt that I was in heaven indeed. The feeling that came to my heart then was: Oh! if I could live worthy, though it would require fourscore years, so that in the end, when I have finished I could go into His presence and receive the feeling that I then had in His presence, I would give everything that I am and ever hope to be!" (*Melvin J. Ballard-Crusader for Righteousness*, Salt Lake City, Utah: Bookcraft Inc., 1966, p. 66.) This is what Jesus Christ is inviting each of us to experience.

Every person who speaks about this sacred experience will testify that it was the most important event in their life and that they would pay any price to be worthy of its continuation. Elder George F. Richards expressed such feelings of resolve and commitment after the Savior appeared to him. He said, "I was in the presence of my Savior as He stood in mid-air . . . My love for him was such that I have not words to explain . . . As a result of that dream, I had this feeling that no matter what might be required at my hands . . . I would do what I should be asked to do even to the laying down of my life . . . If only I can be with my Savior and have that same sense of love I had in that dream, it will be the goal of my existence, the desire of my life." (*Ensign*, May 1974, p. 119.)

Many feel that such experiences are not for the "ordinary" member, but are reserved for the apostles and prophets alone. This is not true. The Lord said the invitation applies to every soul and he meant exactly that. (See

D&C 93:1.) A pioneer named Alexander Neibaur testified on his death bed, "I have seen my Savior. I have seen the prints in his hands. I know that Jesus is the Son of God, and I know that this work is true and that Joseph Smith was a prophet of God. (*Historical Magazine*, 5:52, as cited in *Ensign*, August 1975, p. 19.)

Alfred Douglas Young, an "ordinary" member of the church, saw the Savior September 17th, 1841. Feeling drawn by the Spirit, he left a gospel discussion in his brother's home and went into the woods where he could have privacy. He was met by an angel who said, "Follow thou me." Alfred said, "He ascended upward in the direction from whence he came and I followed him. He took me into the presence of God the Father and his Son Jesus Christ . . . I saw them seated on a throne . . . I bowed myself on my knees on the altar in front of me which was also in front of the throne. I prayed to God the Father in the name of his Son Jesus Christ to accept the offering I had laid upon the altar . . . Jesus arose and stepped from the side of his Father and came near where I stood. I was in their presence and I gazed upon their glory. Jesus then said to me, 'Your offering is accepted' ." (*Autobiographical Journal*, 1808-1842, pp. 3-13, as quoted in *Ensign*, August 1975, p. 2.)

In our own time, President Harold B. Lee testified, "I know that Jesus Christ lives, and that he's closer to this Church and appears more often in holy places than any of us realize excepting sometimes to those to whom he makes personal appearance." (*Living Prophets For a Living Church*, Church Educational System, 1974, p. 119.)

We have emphasized throughout this book that it is not the mistakes of the past which concern our Savior as much as what we have learned and become through our experience and tests. While it is no small thing to commit sin, for the consequences and the path back is difficult, nothing we sincerely repent of and obtain forgiveness for can prevent us from fulfilling the promises described in this chapter. Kerry Fox was a young man who demonstrated the great truth that when one has been cleansed and sanctified through repentance and the Savior's atonement, the past is not only forgiven and forgotten, it is irrelevant.

Kerry found his way into the Savior's arms of love shortly before he died at the age of twenty-seven. Let me tell you why that is so significant.

Kerry was raised in a strong LDS family, but at the age of thirteen he drifted away from the church. As soon as he was old enough to leave his family, Kerry moved to California where he became quite successful in a career of modeling and TV commercials. Without the strengths of the gospel to protect him, he fell into many sins. He later explained it this way: "For someone who had grown up with a self-image of being thin and unattractive, this was like a dream come true. I indulged myself completely and took every worldly pleasure that came my way, drawing me further and further from the gospel. I was jetted to exotic foreign lands, chauffeured by limousine to black tie dinners and supplied with all the champagne and recreational drugs my body could tolerate."

But the fast, easy money and whirlwind popularity did not last. As the work tapered off, Kerry found himself deep in debt and abandoned by those he thought were his friends. He became angry and bitter. He began drinking heavily and became deeply involved in cocaine and other drugs as a means of escape. Unable to pay his debts, Kerry was almost beaten to death. He was found in his empty apartment only semi-conscious. His jaw had been badly broken and both of his arms were broken.

As he lay in the hospital recovering, pondering the hollowness of his life, Kerry cried out to his Heavenly Father for the first time in many years. That cry did not go unheeded, and the Lord sent people into Kerry's life who could lead him back to the gospel. As he took the discussions from the missionaries and began reading the Book of Mormon, he gained a new perspective which he said helped him to understand "the importance, the very basis of the role Jesus Christ plays in the gospel message and should play in our individual lives." He said, "Life took on a new meaning for me and, for the first time in my life, I was fulfilled. As I look back now, I realize that I never developed a strong testimony based upon my personal relationship with my Savior, because I never took the time to understand that key point of the gospel."

Then, after finding himself and making his life right with the Lord, Kerry began losing weight at a rapid pace. The doctors diagnosed him as having a terminal case of Crohn's disease, a cancer of the colon. How thankful he was to have returned to the Lord and completed his repentance *before* he discovered he was going to die. As the cancer spread throughout his body, he endured terrible pain. After six months of unsuccessful therapy the doctors discovered Kerry was also afflicted with AIDS. There was nothing they could do to prevent his rapidly approaching death.

Like the Bible's prodigal son, Kerry had returned home to repair his life. After a long, difficult path of repentance Kerry was ordained an elder, received his endowments in the Salt Lake temple and received a Patriarchal Blessing which promised his sins were forgiven and that he would fulfill an important role as a missionary in the spirit world.

Kerry's mind frequently traveled back over the mistakes of the past and he wondered what his status was with the Lord. Approximately two months before he died, the Lord chose to give Kerry a powerful assurance of his love. These are the words he wrote after meeting the Savior face to face:

> One night while still at home, my temperature rose dangerously. We prayed as a family and decided not to go to the hospital, that if I were to die, I should do so at home. After a blessing by my father, my heart became very warm and still and I began to visualize myself traveling through a tunnel toward a bright light. It was a peaceful feeling, very pleasant. In fact, I felt the room was filled with spirits from the Spirit World.

> As I reached the end of this tunnel, I saw two outstretched arms, which I took and embraced. As I looked up into the face of this being, I came to know that it was Jesus Christ, Himself. I was embracing the Savior! I just melted into all the love and light that He emanated.

> Then he looked me in the face, with tears in His eyes, and said, "You see, I do exist. I needed you to know."

I just wept with joy and we stood and embraced for some time. Then he took my hand and pointed me back to the tunnel, saying, "Not yet. You've work to do still."

I began to travel back through the tunnel of light. I opened my eyes to see my father. Tears were streaming down his face, and he said, "Welcome home."

I told my father that it wasn't going to happen tonight and he smiled and said he knew.

Shortly before Kerry died, he wrote the story of his life in the hope it would help others prevent the mistakes that cost him such suffering and grief. His parents have given permission to repeat some of Kerry's story here. He closed his testimony with these words:

I have a testimony of the truthfulness of the gospel. I know that Christ lives. I've been embraced by him. And I know that the prophets and apostles that serve are each called of God. This is true. I can never deny it in this world or in the world to come. Please hearken unto my words and be touched by the Spirit to know that this is true. It's one of the reasons the Lord sent me back to earth, to relay my story. (From an unpublished account of Kerry's life.)

I regret that I never met Kerry. I love him. I think he would have liked us to read the words of another prodigal:

Behold, who can glory too much in the Lord? Yea, who can say too much of his great power, and of his mercy, and of his long-suffering towards the children of men? Behold, I say unto you, I cannot say the smallest part which I feel.

Who would have supposed that our God would have been so merciful as to have snatched us from our awful, sinful, and polluted state? (Alma 26:16-17.)

The time will come when every member of the church will have the opportunity to meet Christ face to face. For some it comes during mortality. Others must wait until we cross the veil. But sooner or later, if we prepare for it with all our hearts, every disciple will have the opportunity to meet our Savior face to face and feel the embrace of the arms of his love.

Shortly before he died, Elder Bruce R. McConkie rose from his sick bed to bear a final testimony in General Conference. I wept as I heard him testify, "I am one of his witnesses and in a coming day I shall feel the nail marks in his hands and in his feet and shall wet his feet with my tears. But I shall not know any better then than I know now that he is God's almighty Son. That he is our Savior and Redeemer and that salvation comes through his atoning blood and in no other way." (*Ensign*, May 1985, p. 11.)

Every disciple of Christ has been invited to experience this same certainty and testimony. But to be part of this fellowship, we must long for it, reach for it, dream of it, keep it alive in our hearts and someday it will be ours.

> And whosoever shall believe in my name, doubting nothing, unto him will I confirm all my words, even unto the ends of the earth. (Mormon 9:25.)

> Let us draw near with a true heart in full assurance of faith. (Hebrews 10:22.)

Epilogue

We have studied the majesty of our Savior's divine personality as described in scripture from the time of Adam through our current prophet.

Before we part, it is essential to realize that the Christ of scripture is the same person with the exact same attributes today. "For I know that God is not . . . a changeable being; but he is unchangeable from all eternity to all eternity," and "I say unto you he changeth not; if so he would cease to be God." (Moroni 8:18; Mormon 9:19.)

If we would open our hearts to the Savior, we must overcome our preoccupation with what he did in the past, so that we may recognize that he is trying to do the very same things for us today.

> For do we not read that God is the same yesterday, today, and forever, and in him there is no variableness neither shadow of changing?" (Mormon 9:9.)
>
> God's attitude toward mankind remains forever the same, his feelings toward us are unchanging and full of love, kindness, and patience. (Hans B. Ringger, *New Era*, November 1987, p. 7.)

Jesus Christ has labored almost six thousand years to convince us of His love. Now, as we conclude this book, we must each answer some questions.

- Can I open my heart and say yes to that incredible love?
- Will I allow him to 'encircle' me in the arms of his love?
- Can I imagine to myself that I hear the voice of the Lord, saying unto me, in that day: "Come unto me ye blessed, for behold, your works have been the works of righteousness upon the face of the earth"? (Alma 5:16.)

In harmony with Alma's challenge, Elder David B. Haight has said, "If we could feel or were sensitive even in the slightest to the matchless love of our Savior and his willingness to suffer for our individual sins, we would cease procrastination and 'clean the slate,' and repent of all our transgressions." (*Ensign*, May 1988, p. 23.)

Five of the most wonderful words in all of scripture are: "to go no more out." That is the Father's promise to those who attain exaltation in his celestial kingdom, for "he has also said that the righteous shall sit down in his kingdom, to go no more out." (Alma 34:36.) We know that Heavenly Father and Christ work unceasingly on our behalf, to bring our souls, "yea, [our] immortal souls, [to] the right hand of God in the kingdom of heaven, to sit down with Abraham, and Isaac, and with Jacob, and with all our holy fathers, to go no more out." (Helaman 3:30.)

So another question we must ask ourselves is, "Am I committed to so live my life that I will have the right to go no more out?"

Robert D. Hales said, "As a father, I put my arms around each of my boys as they left to serve their missions and whispered in their ears, 'Return with honor.' I can picture our Father in Heaven putting his arms around each of us as we left his presence and whispering, 'Return with honor.'" (*Ensign*, May 1990, p. 41.)

Let us also ask ourselves, "Am I living so as to return to my Heavenly Father with honor?

Recently our family went to the airport to welcome one of our daughters home from her mission in Chile. For almost two years the highlight of each week was receiving Tracy's letter, rejoicing in her successes and sorrowing with her in the disappointments of people who turned away from the Savior's invitation. But the anticipation we felt each week as we waited for the arrival of her letters was nothing compared to what we felt at the airport as we awaited the arrival of her plane.

There was also another family there waiting to welcome their missionary home. Although we arrived over an hour early, they were there ahead of us, waiting anxiously. With all our balloons and ten foot "welcome home" signs, our two families dominated the deplaning area. Between our two groups there were many children, brothers and sisters, parents, even aunts, uncles and close friends who surrounded the door through which the passengers would enter the terminal.

How earnestly we peered through the windows, watching each plane land, and wondering if that was *the* plane our loved one was on. How anxiously we listened for the arrival announcement of our flight number.

Finally the plane arrived and we watched it park at our terminal. Emotions rose to a high pitch of excitement. How slowly the disembarking tunnel made its way to the door at the front of the plane. Couldn't they hurry a little bit faster? Didn't they know how we had waited and longed for this day when our daughter, no longer a little girl, came back to us after having gone into a far corner of the Lord's kingdom and fought the good fight?

The door opened. People walked toward us. Cameras were ready. Hearts were yearning. Here came the Elder the family in front of us was waiting for. They broke through the barriers and ran to him. There was no waiting patiently once their boy was in sight. Mother made it first, then father and a crowd of loved ones, all reaching toward him with hungry arms, eager to touch, eager to affirm their love and welcome him home.

Then finally, the one we waited for appeared. We too ran, unashamed to show the joy we felt in her honorable return. Hugs just weren't enough. Over and over we said how much we loved her, how proud we were of her, and most of all, WELCOME HOME, Tracy. She could hardly walk for the way we crowded around her, yearning to be close and assure her of our love.

Others flowed from the plane unnoticed, wondering I am sure, what all the fuss was about. If only they knew. Our daughter was home! She had been gone so long. Every day of her absence was filled with our longing and prayers for her success and return with honor. And now, at last she was ours again. How could those strangers possibly know what this reunion meant to the fulfillment of our love and anticipation of this long-awaited day?

As I have reflected on this occasion, the Spirit has whispered to me that the emotions of that sacred occasion were only a tiny glimpse into the reunion that will one day take place as each of us passes back through the veil that has separated us from our Heavenly Mother and Father. For that glad reunion they will have waited our entire mortal lives. The Savior himself will greet us personally. As Neal A. Maxwell said,

> There the self-assigned gatekeeper is Jesus Christ, who awaits us out of a deep divine desire to welcome us as much as to certify us. Hence, "He employeth no servant there." (2 Nephi 9:14.)
>
> If we acknowledge Him now, he will lovingly acknowledge and gladly admit us then! (*Notwithstanding My Weakness*, Salt Lake City, Utah: Deseret Book, 1981, p. 124.)

Can we dream of that reunion? Can we long for it as our Savior, Heavenly Father and Mother do? Can we anticipate it every day of our lives? If we will live for it, yearn for it, keep it alive in our minds and hearts, then someday it will come to pass. And then we will know the unimaginable joy of melting into our Heavenly Parents' arms, with the assurance that we will be forever in their presence and share in the perfect joys of eternity.

Index of Illustrative Stories

Topical Index